THE
DAILY UNDOING

Being Better at Being Human

DAVID GAUDET

Contributor: Marc Boivin
Cover Artist: Nadia Perna

The Daily Undoing: Being Better at Being Human
Copyright © 2021 by David Gaudet

Tellwell Talent
www.tellwell.ca

ISBN
978-0-2288-5137-0 (Hardcover)
978-0-2288-5136-3 (Paperback)
978-0-2288-5138-7 (Ebook)

CONTENTS

To Anne-Marie, Eva, Gabby, and Tommy; forever lighting my journey of being better at being human.

ACKNOWLEDGEMENTS

I have co-authored or contributed to five textbooks in circulation in North America but, aside from writing and being deftly poked and prodded by various editors, I have zero experience in taking a book from start to finish. Until now. While "The Daily Undoing" podcast was pre-designed to have an accompanying workbook for release in late 2020, I admittedly didn't get my head into that second part until, well, late 2020. It seems producing a daily podcast runs counter to getting much else accomplished.

I hastily began rifling through the hundreds of scripts I had written to produce the actual podcast and started the arduous task of refining them to be, short, punchy, actionable and, "book-friendly." In the meantime, my frequent collaborator, University of Calgary professor, competency-based learning thought leader, and contributor to this book, Marc Boivin offered to condense all of his research, synthesizing what all this competency stuff really meant, why it was worth knowing, and how it would be woven throughout this book. Once Marc had finished laying the foundation of the front sections of this book, he nobly and generously undertook the task of reviewing and editing all 366 daily entries! I am grateful to Marc for his generosity, intellectual depth, strategic insight, and friendship.

After developing a couple of mock-up pages, I sent samples to a trusted circle of colleagues, students, professionals and entrepreneurs who had a) been loyal to listening to the podcast, and b) would be brutally honest with me in sharing their opinion as to whether this book idea had any merit. I'd like to thank that first focus group for helping to guide me early on.

Matthew Boudreau	Trevor Huggins	Courtney Thorne
Rhonda Choate	Emily Jesse	Anne-Marie Turski
Gord Choate	Kim Lawrence	Bonnie Vandersteen
Chelsey Dalzell	Robin Moffat	Shauna Vowel
Alexis Hood	Amie Plourde	Jason Zaran

As the look and feel of the workbook pages were evolving, I appealed to Nadia Perna, an amazing young graphic artist, attending the Alberta University of the Arts, in Calgary, for assistance. I had mocked up a cover concept myself but when I stepped back to look at it, I was convinced it needed to be more striking. I had barely described a vague theme before Nadia had emailed the first version of the cover art. She's brilliant, and my gratitude goes to her for creating the visual statement I feel this book cover makes. She also designed the icon system used throughout the book to help you navigate between the competencies.

While the self-publishing industry is alive and well, and relatively easy to enter, there's still a lot of expected, and unexpected, turbulence that only a veteran can pilot through safely. At the last minute, I found Sonia Marques on Upwork, who made herself available for a Zoom call on short notice and proceeded to reassure me that she was that page layout pilot I sought. Turns out my rather "simple" page layout required some fairly tedious manual hacks, of which she performed diligently and patiently.

In the final stages of completing the book, I needed a true professional to sweep through it. Someone who would sniff out everything from grammatical errors, to missing periods, to properly attributing my sources. Moreover, this person had to be blunt, and unafraid of offending me. For this I made a last minute plea to a colleague with whom I had worked on previous textbooks – freelance Content Development Manager, Courtney Thorne. It's fair to say her expertise and efficiency were a godsend.

I would be remiss if I did not acknowledge those who have supported The Daily Undoing podcast over the years as well. Being holed up in my makeshift basement studio for hours on end in the wee morning hours to produce something like this often begs the question, "Why?" But it was the random, unsolicited messages from friends and perfect strangers acknowledging the value the messages had delivered to them, that were often a much-needed source of motivation.

Finally, the people closest to me are the ones to whom I am the most grateful. My wife Anne-Marie and our children Eva and Gabby put up with the insane work schedule required for this project, which consumed untold hours throughout the year 2020 and well into 2021. This book was made possible not only because of their tolerance of my fluctuating moods and sleep-deprived lack of presence, but also because of the promise I see in my daughters and the way my wife has insisted we raise them. Anne-Marie also deserves indescribable credit for a multitude of roles, ranging from reviewer, editor, overall compass-checker, strategist, and morale booster.

All of these inputs and inspirations conspired to form and flesh out the many thoughts contained in The Daily Undoing podcast, and in the pages that follow.

—David Gaudet

FOREWORD

In 2016, I entered the second year of my bachelor's degree in business at the Southern Alberta Institute of Technology (SAIT), Calgary, AB. With my first year and 10 courses completed, I thought I had figured out how to adjust to the changing styles of my professors. That's when I walked into my first day of *Brand Management* and met my new professor David Gaudet. From the moment he introduced himself, you could feel there was going to be a different tone in his class from all the other professors. For the first time we did not have someone regurgitating information at us, but rather asking us questions on our views, perceptions, likes and dislikes about the world around us. This was Dave's way of teaching us *how* to learn and not just *what* to learn. And it was my first experience of competency-based learning.

Over the following years, Dave fostered relationships with students, myself included. He invested in our well-being as students, with genuine interest in how he could contribute to our academic success. But he also took interest in us as human beings and was quick to show empathy and compassion while challenging us to reach higher and further.

Before my final year at SAIT, Dave and Marc Boivin were conducting focus groups on the first book they had written together, *Mindtap for Marketing* and I was able to see first-hand how this competency-based learning could be integrated into any subject matter. These difficult-to-teach competencies like critical thinking, communication, collaboration, and creativity were woven into the marketing theory and integrated into the way their book would be delivered – using activities that would secure knowledge, while ensuring skills could be demonstrated. These were the key components, as I would come to know, of a competency-based framework.

Now, looking back a few years after my graduation, with experience working in the marketing profession, I certainly appreciate the business theory I learned at SAIT. Though I can't say every lesson I learned in school has stuck with me, I can say without a doubt the way David taught us *how to learn,* using these life competencies, and the methods behind them, have become habitual in my work and indispensable to my success.

—Emily Jesse
Southern Alberta Institute of Technology; Alumni

FROM PODCAST TO PRINT

The Daily Undoing began as an experiment in the summer of 2018. I had been out for a run, listening to Gary Vaynerchuk's *Crushing It* when he came to the final chapter, "Voice-First." In it, he described how mini-podcasts could be shared via smart speakers and, in true "Gary Vee" form, asserted that this was a place where all marketers needed to be in their never-ending search for attention.

Sweat-soaked, I jumped online to research this new avenue of communication, decided that Amazon's Alexa platform would be the easiest point of entry, and about an hour later had submitted my first Alexa "Flash Briefing" (Amazon terminology for these mini-podcasts) to Alexa for review. A few hours after that, *The Daily Undoing* was live. Of course, the only way it would be heard would be by sheer accident but that didn't matter. Both me and my kids got the biggest kick out of shouting, "Alexa, What's My Flash Briefing?!" and having my voice come out of our Echo speaker.

By October of that year, I was off to the races, writing, recording and publishing an episode of the flash briefing Monday to Friday. Subject matter varied, from contrarian views on education and marketing – the worlds in which I spend most of my professional life – to providing different perspectives on news events. So enthusiastic was I about the work-flow I had developed to produce flash briefings, that I had actually introduced Alexa Flash Briefings as a term project in my *Innovation and Design* course in the Southern Alberta Institute of Technology's Bachelor of Business Administration program. But beyond that, nobody, other than me, my children and my somewhat confused students, were giving The Daily Undoing much notice.

It finally came to my attention that, despite Vaynerchuk's prediction, the world was not embracing flash briefings quite as quickly as I had hoped. I found myself, more often than not, explaining my rather time-consuming hobby as simply "podcasting" and had by then found a way to channel the content onto the most popular podcast players – Apple Podcasts and Spotify.

Months passed, and with each milestone crossed – 100 episodes, 200 episodes – people kept asking "what is the purpose?" and "how do you make money from it?" The person asking this question the most was yours truly. By spring 2019 I had drained hundreds of hours towards my little "hobby," and, while it had given a voice to a movement my partner Marc Boivin and I were trying to rouse, there was still little notice given to it, and nary a dime in revenue generated. While a random cursory thought may have been given to actually marketing the podcast, I was too busy making it to do much else. Oh, and I had also hitched the wagon of the podcast to the hope that social media would bring it greater attention - secretly but naively imagining that somehow, through the abyss of Instagram, my content would magically grow a fanbase.

By the end of 2019, I came to the conclusion that, a) I still had no idea what I was trying to accomplish with The Daily Undoing, and b) I would have to find its purpose or pull the plug. Hobbies are nice but this one was far too draining, and was providing less and less a feeling of personal satisfaction. All of which would have been tolerable if I had bothered to seek and secure a sponsor. At least then I'd be motivated to serve that advertiser. But as things stood at that time, I had little to show for untold, unpaid, hours of "experimenting."

In the waning days of 2019, I made the rather unoriginal decision to "make changes in my life next year," spurred mostly by my podcast dilemma. By this time, my aforementioned collaborator Marc Boivin and I had begun getting sharper with the focus of our joint endeavor as well. The "Undoing" part of the podcast's name, it should be noted, had become the symbol of this abstract and undefined project he and I had been working on. Kind of like the podcast, we felt an invisible pull toward something, but had little more to go on than a hunch that something was there and that it was worth pursuing. The foundation for this otherwise undefined venture, however, was the concept of Competency-Based Learning (CBL).

After Marc and I had been introduced to work on a textbook project together, we discovered that we shared many things in common, including a propensity to teach business through activities versus strictly through theory, and that those activities inevitably flowed through a framework of non-technical skills. Curiosity, critical thinking, collaboration, creativity, etc., were things we had forced our students to practice while in the process of learning about marketing, economics, management, accounting and so on. Importantly, we had also discovered through primary and secondary research, that industry had collectively identified a concerning trend of incoming graduates. That they often lacked these vital workplace competencies. Workplace competencies, it turned out, just weren't being taught. So determined were we to implement this philosophy that we insisted this activity-driven learning method become the underpinning of that first textbook we wrote, *Mindtap for Marketing* published by Nelson Education Ltd. in 2017.

While together we would meander down endless rabbit holes, peeking and poking at things we felt we could "disrupt" in education. We were first and foremost fathers and educators who were having a difficult time wedging this Undoing "thing" into our lives. Was it, like the podcast, a hobby? Or was it a business, awaiting the arrival of a rather necessary, but elusive, business model?

So I had both a non-descript podcast and, if it were possible, an even more non-descript business hanging over me like a dense fog, but I was convinced there lay abundant light and clarity above it. I decided quite quickly that the two worlds could be brought together in a podcast whose purpose would be…wait for it…evangelizing competencies! I could hear the crickets even in the dark deafening quiet of my mind. It was neither the most sexy, nor easy-to-explain theme for a podcast, but I persuaded myself that it was a theme worth knowing, a story worth telling, and, at the very least, it was a direction of some kind.

However, it was a direction without a path, or even much of an identity. Sure, academics decades before had introduced and legitimized CBL as a pedagogical concept, and it had made inroads with HR departments of various forward-thinking businesses. But it remained a rather abstract and misunderstood idea. How in the world was I going to give it a voice in daily 60 second podcast episodes, and more importantly, who would care? But this, to me, became the point of it all. It was an untold story, ensnared and seemingly stuck in academia, that needed a mainstream voice. It wasn't just for academia and HR departments. It was for everyone. These competencies were innate in all of us, just sitting there, mostly dormant, requiring conscious stimulation in order to deliver their endless value.

The Daily Undoing, Season 2, would give clarity to these vital yet underused behaviours possessed by us all, and if it awakened this reality to a single person, then it would be worth it. The podcast would regularly amplify these competencies as a collection of secret super-powers – in turn making them less secret. My framework and work process would be simple. Each day, in sixty second mini podcasts, I would discuss one of what I called, eight "Pillar Competencies," and rotate them throughout the entire year. These competency categories were:

1. Curiosity
2. Creativity
3. Problem solving
4. Collaboration
5. Communication
6. Character
7. Citizenship
8. Critical thinking

Within each one of these categories I would attach a different action-word that would connect the competency to a daily activity. These would be broadcast every day on Apple Podcasts, Spotify, and Alexa, as well as on Instagram, Facebook, and Linkedin, using graphical posts to emphasize the action-word of the day. Oh, and here's where you come in, my most appreciated reader. The scripts used for *The Daily Undoing* podcast would somehow be morphed into a workbook, to be published at the end of the year. How I would do this, I decided, was a minor detail, I'd work out later...

On January 1, 2020, the *Daily Undoing* began a 366-day (leap year) journey, describing, demonstrating and unleashing the power of competencies to anyone who cared. Of course, no one expected COVID 19 to turn the world upside down two months in, but one thing about competencies is that they are your resource to leverage in good times and bad. This is where the journey took a somewhat profound turn for better or worse. What I had intended to be a collection of thoughts and activities, unbound to a specific time period, instead had organically fused to this much bigger unfolding story. Thus, *The Daily Undoing* podcast became a pseudo-chronicle of an unforgettable year in human history, weaving the practical use of competencies against the backdrop of a global pandemic, racial injustice, a US presidential election that never seemed to end, and various other topics that trickled on to the radar.

With the world seemingly becoming more and more unhinged by the day, any time felt like a good time to jump ship and shelf the project until everything was "back to normal" – a phrase I'm sure began to nauseate you as much as it did me. But by this time, I was addicted to the process, which had begun to create in me an unexpected higher sense of purpose.

I had ritualized the podcast into my life, feeling that the ensuing chaos was actually amplifying the need to be aware of the power of competencies. The unplanned change of course would eventually result in two conflicting consequences. On one hand, it made for a more interesting real-time podcast, likely drawing interest and attention if only for the fact that it was there every day, when nothing seemed certain. On the other hand, it was going to be difficult, if not impossible, to re-use what was now, very time-bound content, in a book intended to be read and applied more generically for years to come.

As I began sorting through this dilemma in October 2020, mulling through the hundreds of podcast scripts, it became clear that, in a year marked by billions of individual pivots, I too would need my own. The scripts, I thought, served their purpose in real time, but now their "time-boundedness" had to be removed for the workbook to work. But this felt like a compromise. As the year wore on, each podcast episode became a running chronicle of the contrasting stories that were unfolding. Through one lens, tragedy of unimaginable scale. Through another, humanity and hope, many might have thought unattainable by a human race assumed to have long since become detached, desensitized, and de-humanized. It seemed somehow counter-intuitive to keep the many twists, turns, storylines, and subplots out of the workbook, and yet that very narrative seemed starkly out of context for this type of book.

To add to the conundrum, many of those involved in the market testing of the book thought the time-bound references in the podcast were too important to leave out. My remedy for this was to separate the podcast from print, but at the same time, to provide that critical connection for those interested in accessing the bigger picture.

To that end, as you read through *The Daily Undoing* work pages that follow, you'll note each has the word "Episode" and a number, at the top of the page. Thus, "Episode 1," "Episode 2" all the way through "Episode 366." These numbers correspond with the episode numbers of *The Daily Undoing*, podcast, Season 2 on Apple Podcasts. Plus, beyond the podcast reference, I began to think "episode" was just a way cooler way to think of how life sort of plays itself out.

As explained, these are not typical podcasts. They are bite-sized, sixty second briefs, so will not require prolonged periods of time to digest. In the vast majority of the podcast episodes, the connection is pretty obvious with the content in the following pages. For a variety of reasons, there are rare cases where *The Daily Undoing* entry in this book goes slightly off script from the podcast version. However, for the most part, the context and the backdrop of the year 2020 breathes through the words shared via the podcast – hope, humanity, tragedy, Black Lives Matter, Trump, and anything else that shaped a truly remarkable year. You'll also hear shout-outs to national and international personalities, or local Calgary entrepreneurs, in cases where normal folks or new-found heroes could be used to demonstrate how to practice being more competent looked, and how *being better at being human* mattered.

THE PROBLEM WITH COMPETENCIES

OK, I'll be the first to admit, as a marketing educator and branding nerd, there is an inherent problem with words like "competent" and "competency" in their ability to stir up much excitement as the theme of a book, much less bear the burden of branding a *movement*. Truth is, Marc Boivin, CBL researcher and speaker, and I have had many a tussle with the nomenclature of this beyond its rightful place in educational methodology. With *The Daily Undoing*, I was going to attempt to bring this to the mainstream. But of all the heights to which one can aspire, why in the world would they aspire to be "merely" competent? The word, frankly, reeks of mediocrity. Imagine, for example, "Steve, the competent plumber." Not exactly the kind of eye-grabbing words to paint on the side of a service van.

And so we spent weeks attempting to come up with a shiny, new term. One that, like an awesome brand name, would act like an instant super-charged attention magnet. The problem was that none of those words captured the essence of competency in the context of learning – which is ultimately what *The Daily Undoing* was supposed to be about, and precisely why the word is essential in the label, *competency-based learning*. It is a mindset for learning, which in turn becomes a foundation for personal growth. In the many talks Marc and I have given at conferences across North America, words like "mastery" and "credentials" are often floated around as though there should be some end goal in this abstract pursuit of competency. But the truth is, there is no end goal. Like our capacity for pure thought, there is no limit, no maximum, no mastery. There is only, if one is willing to embrace it, a lifelong *pursuit* of mastery.

Besides the potential limitations of "competency" from a branding perspective, the next challenge with the word is the natural synonymous association so often made between competency, and one of its component parts – skill. Decades ago, the distinction was made between technical skills (ranging from STEM subjects to trades) and soft skills – sometimes, albeit inaccurately, used interchangeably with interpersonal skills. While I still cringe at the vernacular of "soft" and "skills" fused together, the intention was always to distinguish a set of skills which were largely intangible, but equally essential in careers and life. Either way, however, "skill" also has limitation in its meaning. It is possible, for instance, to be skilled at something, without being fully knowledgeable about it. Conversely, it is possible to be knowledgeable without being skilled. As Marc often opines, "We don't give out driver's licenses based upon written exams."

Thus, competency-based learning attempts to reconcile the deficiencies of both skill and knowledge by making them part of a learning system, along with one other essential ingredient – attitude. That is, conscious openness and willingness to learn must be omnipresent in order for us to continue becoming more competent. As you'll read throughout the book, and hear often in the podcast, *The Daily Undoing* frequently mirrors the entrepreneurial mindset – an attitude willing to learn; to fail; to make sacrifices; to challenge and, to always ask.

What makes competencies compelling for educators like me and Marc is that there is an assumption that learning involves more than just information transfer. Competency-based learning is both a framework and mindset that sets those who embrace it on a lifelong journey of learning to learn. We may think we know it all, have learned it all, and can do it all, but our capacity to learn is infinite. As Albert Einstein quipped, "The more I learn, the more I realize how much I do not know." There may be no greater endorsement for a competency-based approach to learning, and to life, than this single, solitary thought.

The fact that you hold this book in your hands, and have read it to this point is a strong suggestion that you possess the ***attitude*** required for this journey. What this book attempts to do is make you more aware of the vast stores of ***knowledge*** and wisdom you possess, across eight different competency categories, and suggest multiple ***skills*** to perform consciously, regularly, and willingly, in your journey toward being better at being human. So, there really is no problem with the words *competency* or *competent*. There is only a problem with the general assumption that we are forever and fully competent in the areas emphasized in this book. That we can conjure these competencies on-demand, assuming high performance without practice. *The Daily Undoing* seeks to help solve this problem.

HOW TO USE THIS BOOK

As you seek greater competency across the eight categories in this book, it might help to have a framework in mind to which you can identify and organize a competency's three ingredients: Attitude, Knowledge and Skill (AKS Framework). For that may I present every educator's best friend, the Venn diagram, which is present on each action page of *The Daily Undoing*.

Figure 1: Competency AKS Framework

The letters AKS within the Venn, represent **A**ttitude, **K**nowledge and **S**kill. Full disclosure, I did not invent this framework, any more than I invented the concept of competencies. Like the concept of competency based learning, the AKS framework is in a state of constant evolution, stemming from the work of a vast trail of pioneering researchers, scholars and practitioners. And it is a path marked by ongoing discussion and debate over the exact meaning and construct of competencies. In some circles, for example, the "A" stands for "Ability." Marc and I liked "Attitude" better, so took the liberty to change it. So with humble acknowledgement to those who came before me in developing the whole notion of CBL, and the framework upon which it is learned and leveraged, let's just say, I feel the overall system used here most fits the spirit of a book whose subtitle is "being better at being human." With that said, let's take a closer look at each of these three elements:

1. **Attitude** - the perspective a person has on something, and the feelings that result in that interaction.
2. **Knowledge** - the explicit information that exists on a particular topic and the ability to process and recall that information.
3. **Skill** - the tangible abilities that are displayed by applying knowledge, usually through the completion of certain tasks or activities.

Thus, to be competent, a person has to be able to manage these three elements in a way that allows them to show that they not only understand something, but also can *apply* it to a real-life situation. And while all of this is happening, the person presents a beneficial attitude towards the process and seeks to continually work on improvement. As noted thought leader in human motivation, Daniel Pink, asserts, "Goals that people set for themselves and that are devoted to attaining mastery are usually healthy."

Similarly, the goal of *The Daily Undoing* is not simply to memorize knowledge nor gain a master credential symbolizing a skill. It is to create an internal mental flywheel of high performing competencies from which to draw when the twists and turns of your life's story summons them into action. It is also about attaining a state of mind that you can never attain mastery. You can only commit to its pursuit.

Mastery is elusive, because it is rarely something that can be reached. But it is in the process of working towards mastery where one can start to find the freedom and limitless potential of competency based learning and escape the restrictions of our education and work systems that reward based upon certain designations (e.g., A+, or $5,000 bonus). Instead, to seek competency is to drive towards constant and continual self-improvement, one clear action step at a time.

I thought a lot about all of this when coming up with the book's subtitle. While competency based learning is the foundational theory, my hope for you, as you participate in the pages that follow, is that competency based *learning* is seen as competency based *living*. And when you begin to realize your conscious intention in practicing the eight Pillar Competencies (explained in the next section), using this AKS framework, you should feel a sense of reward not for being perfect, but for your ongoing pursuit of *being better at being human*. Grammarians will shudder at that last phrase, arguing it should be, "*be* better at being human." But this is a hair worth splitting. Like competencies, we never arrive at mastery at being human. Our job is to simply continue trying. There should never be a point where we feel, "Okay, I'm better - enough." We should always be "being better," our operating system always updating.

Whether it's learning, living or *being*, these are non-linear concepts. They ebb and flow with moods, personal situations, external forces, in real time. There are a year's worth of daily actions here for you to jump in and out of as time and self-motivation permit. If we have learned anything from 2020, it's that we cannot define ourselves by time in the traditional way. Hours, days, weeks and months are not as important as health, relationships, connections, aspirations and goals. Give yourself permission to pick up and use this companion in a way that fits YOU. While designed as a daily habit-forming exercise, don't punish yourself if you open it only once a week. Conversely, if you wish to bite off more than one exercise in one day – go for it.

DAILY UNDOING ACTION PAGES

The first thing to note is that each page is, in and of itself, an enactment of the competency framework. By turning the page and reading the content you *are*, in fact engaging the required **attitude**. The reading of the competency example on each page is, despite being obvious in many cases, further absorption of **knowledge**. Even if it's just thinking about a word you've used all your life, in a slightly different way. Finally, the action recommended, if performed, completes the framework by exercising a **skill**.

You'll note each page is branded by its respective Pillar Competency's icon in the outer top corner (the description of these comes in the next section). Beside the heading of "Competency" on each page is the specific Pillar Competency to be stimulated and worked on in that page. Immediately beneath that, is a brief perspective, application or insight into the competency. You'll cycle through each of the eight Pillar Competency categories evenly throughout the book, providing a well-rounded diet of these different behavioual areas. Remember, these are all messages from a podcast that ran every day, so there are dozens of different ways to think through and act upon your level of critical thinking, communication, citizenship, etc.

Following "Competency," an "Action" is recommended to give the competency a workout. Some are very specific and quantifiable things, such as being asked to draw or write something, while others are more reflective and thought provoking. Most of the page exists for you to treat the book as though it is unfinished, to be completed by you.

The aforementioned Venn diagram, representing the competency framework, hovers in the background of each page, omni-present, mostly to spur thought, but sometimes directly referenced in the action itself. Either way, you are encouraged to fill the pages with thoughts, contemplations, action tasks, learnings about yourself, or anything else that visibly demonstrates that you're becoming more consciously aware of the bounty of potential inside your own competencies.

In short, each page provides an example of one of the eight competencies, followed by an action on how to apply them. You do not have to follow the action necessarily, but it is a good starting point. You'll begin with a blank canvas, like the one in Figure 2. The framework is designed to look something like Figure 3. However, in the spirit of everything this book stands for, I totally encourage you to create something more like Figure 4 – only M-E-S-S-I-E-R!

You can use the converging circles of the Venn diagram verbatim, by filling in words and doodles that apply to attitude, knowledge and skill (Figure 3), or you can let them just sit in the background as a constant reminder of what you're really working on: becoming more competent, while in turn, being better at being human.

EPISODE 1

COMPETENCY: CURIOSITY

"The Daily Undoing: Being Better at Being Human" is here to awaken eight Pillar Competencies within you. If you're an adult, curiosity is the one competency that's likely been dormant the longest. So let's start there.

ACTION: AWAKEN

In beginning this process you are in fact, already demonstrating curiosity. But what are you curious about?

Figure 2: Blank Action Page

1.
LISTEN TO PODCAST

EPISODE 1

2.
READ

COMPETENCY: CURIOSITY

"The Daily Undoing: Being Better at Being Human" is here to awaken eight Pillar Competencies within you. If you're an adult, curiosity is the one competency that's likely been dormant the longest. So let's start there.

ACTION: AWAKEN

In beginning this process you are in fact, already demonstrating curiosity. But what are you curious about?

3.
SET ATTITUDE

Gut check. I am opening myself up to personal growth.

4.
SEEK TO KNOW

Is my sense of curiosity really asleep? When was the last time I felt curious?

I'm curious about:
- ways to grow
- learning more about myself
- how to be a better leader....
LOL many things!

5.
PRACTICE THE SKILL

Figure 3: Follow AKS Framework

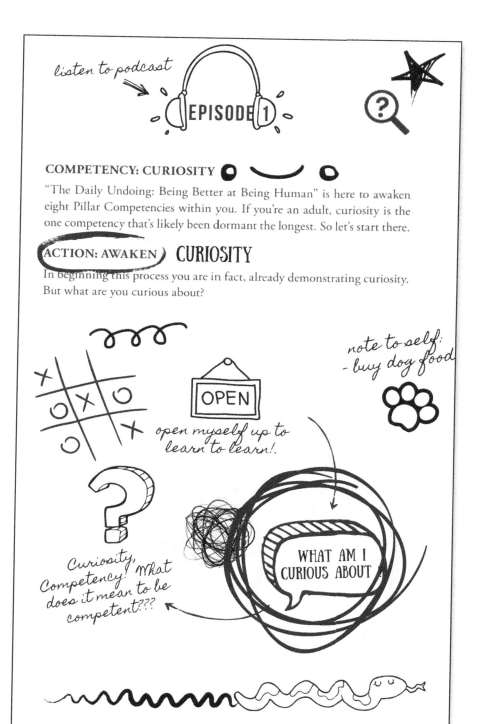

listen to podcast

EPISODE 1

COMPETENCY: CURIOSITY

"The Daily Undoing: Being Better at Being Human" is here to awaken eight Pillar Competencies within you. If you're an adult, curiosity is the one competency that's likely been dormant the longest. So let's start there.

ACTION: AWAKEN CURIOSITY

In beginning this process you are in fact, already demonstrating curiosity. But what are you curious about?

note to self:
- buy dog food

OPEN

open myself up to learn to learn!

WHAT AM I CURIOUS ABOUT

Curiosity, Competency! What does it mean to be competent???

Figure 4: Screw AKS Framework

8 PILLAR COMPETENCIES

Competencies, as I've not so subtly tried to suggest, are a BIG deal. But just to demonstrate the growing embracement of the philosophy, you need look no further than any learning institution or educational branch of government. Each of which, these days, has allocated quite a bit of thought and resources into the subject, and most of which have their own sort of "Top 10" (or 8 or 12 or 19) competencies. In my own province of Alberta, Canada, the Ministry of Education not only echoes the construct of competencies as that which you find here (attitude, knowledge, skill) but also publishes a similar list of what it considers to be the most important competencies. At an international level, the World Economic Forum regularly publishes its research based "most important workplace skills." I know, they're using the "s" word, but when you look at the list, you'll realize they're really talking about competencies – not merely skills. Perhaps I'll send them a copy of this book.

The point is this: educational institutions, governments, global think-tanks and on and on, not only believe in the premise of competencies, but also have generated their own lists of the most important competencies. All of these lists, without exception, include some combination of the following usual suspects:

- Communication
- Collaboration
- Creativity/Design Thinking
- Critical Thinking

Beyond these standard, and absolutely essential competencies, the lists from one entity to another expand, contract, or deviate in some manner, based upon the research brought to the respective table, and consensus arrived at by some "competency jury." I couldn't afford a jury, nor did I feel it necessary. I do not claim my list of "pillar" competencies to be comprehensive, exhaustive, superior, progressive, conservative, liberal, or even original. Although I have yet to find a list of competencies that includes perhaps the most important of them all – curiosity. More on that shortly. There's really no right list or wrong list. It's like coming up with the best rock songs of all time. Everyone's will be slightly different, but the playlists will be interchangeable...not to mention AWESOME by the way! And so, with already way too much ado having been spent, and in no particular order of importance, let me introduce you to the Eight Pillar Competencies woven throughout your workbook.

1. CURIOSITY – THE *ALWAYS BE ASKING* COMPETENCY

We need not start anywhere else, in making the case for curiosity, than Albert Einstein, who humbly confessed, "I have no special talents. I am only passionately curious." As mentioned previously, for whatever reason, the majority of those preceding me in publishing material on competency based learning, have been more inclined to treat curiosity as a required "mindset," but not itself, a competency. I beg to differ.

Curiosity is not only a competency, but it the *gateway competency*. Without a tireless will to know why (and also, what, who, where, when and how) all other competencies in this list are moot. Think about it. How could you possibly think critically without a desire to know not only the views of others, but also the sources of those views. How does creativity stand a chance without a curiosity into understanding what people need and why? How does your communication work if you are devoid of interest in knowing what makes your audience tick? I could go on, but you probably get the point.

Watching the education system slowly erode this essential life competency is harrowing. But making multiple attempts to stimulate your curiosity can help to restore it. As you'll learn from the ideas and activities that follow, many of my thoughts are inspired by really smart people, like Ian Leslie, whose book, *Curious: The Desire to Know and Why Your Life Depends on it* is an indispensable read into the absolute requirement for curiosity in education, work and life. The arguments made in his book are also in alignment with those of the late Sir Ken Robinson and others, so I feel fairly well supported in declaring "curiosity" one of the most important competencies to be strived for in life.

2. CREATIVITY–THE *WILLING TO FAIL* COMPETENCY

I prefer creativity over its more academic-sounding label of "design thinking," although both are used fairly interchangeably in the book. Design thinking also has a process, popularized by Stanford University's famous Hasso Plattner Institute of Design (d.school), which is kind of ironic, because true creativity actually blossoms in the absence of process. Nevertheless, here's a peak at the process:

1. *Empathize* to discover human need
2. *Define* the need specifically
3. *Ideate* to determine alternatives to satisfy the need
4. *Prototype* the innovation into some physical form
5. *Test* to prove (or disprove) concept

While I lean heavily on d.school's model in my "Innovation and Design" course at SAIT, not even Stanford is untouchable to scrutiny. First, as opined previously, curiosity is the logical first step toward creativity. Second, as is the case with curiosity, sometimes we have to get out of our adult heads and back into our toddler heads to realize that pure creativity can only occur when there is no concept of, nor concern about, failure.

Creativity is often referenced in this book as solving problems, which is not to be confused with "problem solving" – a soon to be described separate competency. Creativity is proactive. It is being awake and aware, and foreseeing opportunities to advance and enhance lives. Problem solving, as we'll note later, is reactive. To be drawn upon when bad things happen.

Like curiosity, as your experiences in work and life grow, creativity is often a casualty. But we must bring it off life-support. Finding new approaches to dealing with unique situations is no longer someone else's job, it's yours.

3. **PROBLEM SOLVING** – THE *FIGUREOUTABLE* COMPETENCY

The process you undertake to problem solve changes with the situation that evolves as you grow into roles - from business to parenting. There are dozens of formally established, research-based versions of the problem solving process, ranging anywhere from four to eight steps. Again, I'm choosing to be succinct in my list of steps to problem solve:

1. Identify the problem
2. Generate a list of viable solutions
3. Evaluate solutions and select a solution
4. Implement the solution

As you've learned in life, and will practice again and again in the pages that follow, every problem is unique and yet somehow *figureoutable,* using some configuration of the steps above. And yet, nothing so simple can be considered to be in the ranks of "Pillar Competencies" unless there is a level of complexity involved. In fact, in many realms of higher education, scholarly work and the workplace, it is often termed as "complex problem solving."

Throughout the book you'll be reminded of delicate scenarios in life. Some of them may be fresh in your mind, having experienced them recently, or going through them now. Others may be like your worst fear, you hope to never encounter. Either way, like with all work pages, there will be some suggested action for you to grow and flex your problem-solving muscles.

4. COLLABORATION - THE *DO WELL WITH OTHERS* COMPETENCY

There's an important distinction to be reminded of here and to employ in performing the collaboration exercises throughout the book. You may have sensed it above. So often this competency is dummied down to *"play"* well with others, suggesting that as long as you go with the flow, don't rock the boat, initiate no harm and no foul, then YOU are a competent collaborator. But this just addresses one of two key components of collaboration.

While it is vital that we commit no harm, try our best to get along, etc., ultimately we are recruited into collaborations for what we are able to *do* – our strengths. What we bring to the table. Similarly, we invite others to collaborate with us due to their strengths, which are complementary, if not compensatory to our own limitations.

However collaboration is a very EQ (emotional quotient)-active competency. It requires confidence and humility simultaneously. It requires courage to stand up for what you truly believe, while also being able to admit that there's a go-forward path that might better than your own. And that you are on board, not to follow that path begrudgingly, but with positivity and enthusiasm.

Finally, while collaboration is often framed as a behaviour in which you will ultimately be forced to make compromises, I suggest, as much wiser pioneers in this space like Dr. Stephen Covey would suggest, that you aim instead for synergies, where 1 +1 equals more something than 2.

5. COMMUNICATION – THE *SPEAK AND LISTEN* COMPETENCY

From presentations in a boardroom to the nonverbal cues you give during a family meal, knowing how you communicate and how you can improve can pay off in many ways. Communication graces all lists of "most important competencies," however, it is vital to know, appreciate, and engage in sharpening communications across its vast and entire scope. Communications is much more than receiving and sending information.

In pages that follow, you'll demonstrate how little communications tactics, often overlooked, can have immediate impact on getting noticed, educating an audience, or convincing a potential customer. Similarly, you'll earn a new appreciation of the silent form of communication – listening.

As a marketing nerd, the communication competency has a special place in my heart and head. It is perhaps the easiest competency to develop because, in most of its permutations, it is visual and tangible. Just as one can become a more competent speller or grammarian, one can learn to become a more persuasive writer, speaker and so on.

But our communication competency must also marry awesomeness with authenticity. Competent communicators hide nothing, and share bad news in a way that, at the very least, assures their audience that someone is owning the information flow. *The Daily Undoing* podcast, as mentioned, took place in 2020, a year that, due to the ravaging COVID 19 pandemic, exposed its share of incompetent communications. Lies, exaggerations, finger-pointing and denials were all swirled together wreaking chaos and making matters worse. On the other hand, you had leaders like Alberta's Director of Health, Dr. Deena Hinshaw, or New York Governor Andrew Cuomo, who took their share of ridicule, but stood by their communications philosophy of frequency and candidness.

6. CHARACTER – THE *POWER OF CHOICE*
COMPETENCY

Character holds dual roles as a competency. On one hand it represents the earning and keeping of trustworthiness. Something you strive for all of your life, first with those close to you, then with friends, your work community and so on. It is your moral compass, as identified with the symbol for character.

Again I willingly and gratefully bow to Dr. Stephen Covey, who essentially wrote the book on character, with *7 Habits of Highly Effective People*. Although, to categorize that trail-blazing work in such stark terms alone would be a significant disservice. Do yourself a favor, if you haven't discovered it, *listen* to the audio book. If you prefer reading, then follow that option, but there's something about the good doctor's voice which seems to be able to unforcefully bake his wisdom into your own behaviour.

The second role of the character competency has to do with resilience. Two more of my favorite books come to mind here. Angela Duckworth's *Grit* and Viktor Frankl's *Man's Search for Meaning*. Two very different perspectives of character, two generations apart, but with coalescing themes that celebrate and espouse the human spirit.

So there's this two-pronged balance of inner fortitude and moral conscience united in the character competency, the daily practice of which will not only serve you well, but serve those with whom you come in contact in your journey of being better at being human.

7. CITIZENSHIP – THE *FOR PLANET AND PEOPLE* COMPETENCY

This is another competency found in few other lists. While often acknowledged as a mindset required for surviving and thriving in a modern world, it is included as a pillar competency, largely influenced by my two Gen Z daughters. Or, if I could be more candid, it is influenced by my admission of accountability as a co-creator of the state of the world my generation, and those preceding me, have left for our children to sort out. Seeing the world being handed to them, through the eyes of a parent, can be a sobering and guilt-laden experience indeed.

But you don't have to be a parent to understand the gravity of a global situation that every day seems to teeter on the brink of complete implosion both societally and environmentally. Your citizenship goes far beyond its traditional definition of being your address and country of birth. To develop your citizenship competency will require that you see beyond borders, colours, cultures, ethnicities, genders, ages, income levels, education levels, political beliefs, religious beliefs…and so on (people), while clearly seeing the ramifications of our neglectful and ignorant environmental practices (planet).

And so, when you see this symbol, know that you will be undertaking a challenge, mundane though it may seem, to be an even more active participant in a planet in desperate need of your service. You needn't be Greta Thunberg. You simply have to work at being better.

8. CRITICAL THINKING – THE *OPEN MINDED ALWAYS* COMPETENCY

Perhaps we, as a species, saw no greater challenge to this competency than in 2020. Climate change, racial injustice, democracy, liberty and, of course, a global pandemic all dominated traditional and social media, as well as our everyday conversations. Anchoring oneself to a mindset of objectivity inside the storm of divisive and loud opinions was a gargantuan challenge – reinforcing the need to keep an open mind even and especially when the going gets rough.

But critical thinking is also *careful* thinking. It takes time, focus and a distraction free environment. I'm convinced that even the revered alumni of the great Stoic philosophers would have found it impossible to concentrate, nevermind contemplate, in our day and age. Can you imagine Marcus Aurelius, Epictetus or Seneca coming up with their timeless gems of wisdom in the time-starved, multi-channel madness of the 21st century?

And yet, we somehow must mentally battle through an increasingly noisy, hurried and frantic day to day life. We must then process the macro and the micro information assaulting our minds, make sense of it all, go to work, feed the kids, take care of ourselves etc. And then somehow revisit the crowded space of our consciousness to make appropriate and correct decisions. Wow! For many of these exercises, you may also need to squeeze in some alone time, where I personally have found my sweet spot for critical thinking. Wherever that "place" or state of mind can be found, that's where you'll be most successful in slowing down and really thinking things through.

In a world eager to tell you what to think, you must continually work on *how* YOU think. Being able to not only take in what you see, but also filter it to your world view is now absolutely vital.

YOUR STORY TO WRITE

Some of the descriptions and actions that lie ahead may make you say "Duh?" or "What?" (as in, what does this have to do with anything?). But keep at it. Chip away. Try one activity a day, every other day, or once a week. Use the competency symbols to leaf through the book if you're feeling particularly *incompetent* in a specific area. In fact, as you get used to working through the pages of this book, you will begin to associate the competency with symbol. By the end of the book, the symbol will hopefully come to represent more than just the competency attached to it. It will be the icon that you use towards building and developing a more competent life, which really means, if the spirit of the book is to be fully embraced, *being better at being human.*

As I've tried to outline in the preceding pages, being better at this – our earthly existence – goes beyond being a good person (citizenship and character). It also means that we speak, write, and listen to others more intentionally (communication). We aspire to know more, and to use that knowledge to be more resourceful (curiosity and creativity). And we recognize the true meaning of working together, achieving synergies while sorting through difficulties (collaboration and problem solving).

Before you jump in, remember, there is more detail, background and context available by listening to the sixty second episodes of *The Daily Undoing* podcast, Season 2, on Apple Podcasts. The episode number at the top of each of the following pages corresponds with the episode number of the podcast. If you're looking for a little inspiration, ideation, or motivation, let me take you back to my headspace as I was coming up with these, as a form of my own self-therapy during a very surreal time in human history.

Which brings me to one final admission, confession, or maybe just a proactive answer to a question you're asking. Why listen to me? And it's a good question. Despite being a competency based learning practitioner throughout my 20 year teaching career, speaking its truth at conferences, writing and podcasting about it intentionally, every day for an entire year, I don't see myself as the guru on this or any other topic for that matter. Believe me when I tell you that every single page you're about to read has been a reflection point for me, as I confront my own challenges in being better at being human. So please don't think of me as the expert, and these my "decrees." Instead, think of me, with this book and podcast, as your like minded, and similarly equipped travel companion. Simply nosing and nudging our path forward together.

It's not my intention to tell you *what* to write on these pages. This is our map that has a few guiding principles to light our way. The path to being better is gradual, meaningful and purpose-driven. We control how we handle every situation we face, and we are in control of every page in this book. Use it as a journal, a diary, or a sketchbook. But USE it. Colour outside the lines, scribble, scratch and make a mess. I have only provided an outline. You write the story.

DAILY UNDOING ACTION PAGES

PILLAR COMPETENCY ICONS

 CURIOSITY

 COMMUNICATION

 CREATIVITY

 COLLABORATION

 CRITICAL THINKING

 PROBLEM SOLVING

 CHARACTER

 CITIZENSHIP

EPISODE 1

COMPETENCY: CURIOSITY

"The Daily Undoing: Being Better at Being Human" is here to awaken eight Pillar Competencies within you. If you're an adult, curiosity is the one competency that's likely been dormant the longest. So let's start there.

ACTION: AWAKEN

In beginning this process you are in fact, already demonstrating curiosity. But what are you curious about?

EPISODE 2

COMPETENCY: CREATIVITY

The creativity competency is about solving old problems in new ways. Creativity isn't just thinking outside of the box. It's about removing the box.

ACTION: INNOVATE

Go to your trash or recycling and remove a box of any size. Figure out how to get one more use out of it.

EPISODE 3

COMPETENCY: CRITICAL THINKING

American actor, author and humourist Will Penn Adair Rogers is thought to have said, "Find where people are traveling, and buy land before they get there." Critical thinking involves observing, learning and making informed decisions.

ACTION: OBSERVE

Go to a store or a library, and watch what people are taking from, and leaving on shelves. What does this tell you about "where people are traveling"?

EPISODE 4

COMPETENCY: CHARACTER

The character competency dives deeply into resilience and passion. But ultimately there must first be commitment to self.

ACTION: COMMIT

Open the very last action page of this book. Write to yourself: "(name), I'm going on a journey, but promise to meet you here with a feeling of (_____)." Sign your name beside it.

EPISODE 5

COMPETENCY: COMMUNICATION

While communications experts encourage us to tell stories, we must remember that no story is based on a single character. There are other players, whose voices also need to be heard.

ACTION: LISTEN

Ask someone how they're doing today, but do so with sincerity, using eye contact and empathy. Listen intentionally.

EPISODE 6

COMPETENCY: COLLABORATION

Collaboration isn't always planned. It often occurs randomly between people forced together by circumstance. The collaboration competency is strengthened even through serendipitous human interaction.

ACTION: SUPPORT

Identify and aid a random stranger in need of support. Be mindful also of a small act of support offered you by a stranger, and make sure that you thank them. Write supportive actions below.

EPISODE 7

COMPETENCY: PROBLEM SOLVING

While "getting shit done" is common bravado, we would do well being guided by a slightly more patient mantra called process. This will take more of your time up front, but save you more in the long run.

ACTION: PROCESS

Identify and describe a current problem and a part of it that you need to process further. Then do so, first by writing down some of the problem's trickier components.

EPISODE 8

COMPETENCY: CITIZENSHIP

Citizenship is the competency of individual commitment to global concerns. We have been brought up learning how to first protect ourselves, then family. Now our planet is calling.

ACTION: PROTECT

Examine your daily habits and identify those that you can undo to benefit people or planet. Write them down.

EPISODE 9

COMPETENCY: CITIZENSHIP

It's not that there aren't enough of us to solve the world's problems. The world needs more advocates – believers of causes and implementers of tasks those causes require.

ACTION: ADVOCATE

List some causes you can get behind. Follow them on social media, and add your voice to their movement.

EPISODE 10

COMPETENCY: PROBLEM SOLVING

Problem solving relies on analysis of facts. The word "analyze," comes from ancient Greek; to break apart. Perhaps your problem needs further dissection.

ACTION: ANALYZE

There's no better place to start analysis of a problem than breaking it into the 5 W's. Start with "what is the problem?"

EPISODE 11

COMPETENCY: COLLABORATION

Collaboration presents situations where it is time to lead, and others where it is time to follow. Time to do everything, and time to delegate. But necessary to every collaborative act is one thing: humility.

ACTION: HUMBLE

Humble yourself, by deflecting positive attention away from you, and toward someone with whom you have collaborated. Plan out this action below.

EPISODE 12

COMPETENCY: COMMUNICATION

Master communicators are master storytellers. Their stories embrace, compel, and entrance us, because they draw upon our own very emotions, thereby reflecting our own unique human experience.

ACTIVITY: STORYTELL

Don't just write bland emails, text messages, social media posts, or reports. To whomever is giving you their attention; take them on a journey to which they can relate. Write down the emotions you expect your audience to feel.

EPISODE 13

COMPETENCY: CHARACTER

In "Man's Search for Meaning," Dr. Viktor Frankl asserted that the *"search,"* in his book's title, is our most powerful source of perseverance. As a holocaust survivor, he had significant authority on the topic.

ACTION: PERSEVERE

Search up Viktor Frankl quotes about the meaning of life, and write one down that resonates with you.

EPISODE 14

COMPETENCY: CRITICAL THINKING

In his book, "Thank You For Being Late," Thomas Friedman suggests we view the time we spend waiting for people, as gifted time to be used for deeper thought. Extract the value in this gift.

ACTION: WAIT

While waiting for someone today, don't pull out your phone for aimless distraction. Instead, think critically (carefully) through a big decision you must imminently make. Write that major decision down so that it's top of mind.

EPISODE 15

COMPETENCY: CREATIVITY

The creativity competency helps you spot problems shared by people, then intuitively turns on empathy, to truly understand the needs involved in creating a solution.

ACTION: EMPATHIZE

Ask someone today "what are you feeling?" rather than the standard, "how are you?" Make mental notes of the response and the conversation which follows. Plot out below, some people to whom you wish to ask this question.

EPISODE 16

COMPETENCY: CURIOSITY

In his book "Curious," Ian Leslie describes three levels of curiosity; the innocent wonderings of a youngster (diversive), the studious pursuits of a scholar (epistemic), and the concern toward others of a caring human (empathetic). Your job is to engage them all.

ACTION: ASK

Come up with 3 different questions – one for each level of curiosity.

EPISODE 17

COMPETENCY: CITIZENSHIP

If you could audit your performance as a global citizen, based upon your contribution to global challenges, would you conclude that you are you giving as much as you are taking?

ACTION: SHARE

Do a rough calculation of your citizenship "balance." Then regardless of your result, sacrifice thirty minutes of your time to learn about a problem you can help to solve. Share your concerns on a social medium or in an email to friends.

EPISODE 18

COMPETENCY: COMMUNICATION

Key to Martin Luther King Jr's legacy as a legendary human rights leader, was his knowing his audience, what words resonated, and how to make them come to life.

ACTION: CONNECT

Watch MLK Jr's "I Have a Dream" speech. Note his body language as much as his choice of words and pace of speaking. Think of how you can integrate even a fraction of these into your communication practices.

EPISODE 19

COMPETENCY: COLLABORATION

A competent collaborator knows when it's time to let others lead, and willingly follows, not resentfully, but with an *increased* sense of self security.

ACTION: FOLLOW

Today is about control, and preparing to hand some of it over to someone else. Seek an opportunity to do so. Start with a list below.

EPISODE 20

COMPETENCY: PROBLEM SOLVING

Plato is said to have called *thinking*, the "talking of one's soul to itself." To do this, he used contemplation; long, extended periods of thought devoted to single subjects.

ACTION: CONTEMPLATE

Merriam-Webster defines contemplate; "to view or consider with continued attention." Find a space without distraction and contemplate on a single problem for ten consecutive minutes.

EPISODE 21

COMPETENCY: CHARACTER

In the 2006 film, "March of the Penguins," we witness the amazing lengths, literally, penguins go to nurture a single egg. Nurturing fosters future development. You may not be a penguin, but you are a nurturer.

ACTION: NURTURE

Choose a part of your life which you have under-nurtured, and give it some needed attention.

EPISODE 22

COMPETENCY: CRITICAL THINKING

Critical thinking should be methodical. Arranging elements of a complex situation makes it easier to make sense of those complexities.

ACTION: ARRANGE

Use the space below to arrange elements of a sticky situation into meaningful groupings. Start with people involved, add facts and other things that are known. Use the 3 circles to lay out how you would do this.

EPISODE 23

COMPETENCY: CREATIVITY

The creativity competency focuses on design thinking – coming up with new ways to solve problems. But whether or not a problem even exists is a vital early step.

ACTION: DEFINE

When you or someone else introduces a solution to a problem, ask "why" it is a problem?

EPISODE 24

COMPETENCY: CURIOSITY

A heightened curiosity will serve you well in your communications, where knowing your audience is paramount.

ACTION: DIG

Prior to making an important call or meeting today, dig into the subject being discussed or the person with whom you are meeting. Observe what their reaction is to your digging deeper.

EPISODE 25

COMPETENCY: CITIZENSHIP

Citizenship requires a respect for different opinions, without which, opinions toward one another turn toxic.

ACTION: RESPECT

Write down two differing opinions on a subject, held by you and someone else. Explain in words how you feel the differing opinions have been formed.

EPISODE 26

COMPETENCY: PROBLEM SOLVING

Lack of information disables objectivity and spurs irrational decision making. You cannot succumb to pressure when a problem requires more information before it can be solved.

ACTION: COLLECT

Think about a time when you lost out on an opportunity. Retrace your steps in problem solving to collect any information you may have missed. Determine what you could have done differently.

EPISODE 27

COMPETENCY: COLLABORATION

Collaboration requires contribution, which is more than just giving. It means giving *together*. This subtlety must not be overlooked.

ACTION: CONTRIBUTE

When you feel you've done your part, reach out to those around you and ask what more you can do. Jot down some extra things you could be doing on a current project below.

EPISODE 28

COMPETENCY: COMMUNICATION

The Dickens classic "A Tale of Two Cities" famously begins with "It was the best of times, it was the worst of times…" Magically and instantly, a specific mood is embodied. Words have that power.

ACTION: EMBODY

Commit extra time today to embody a mood in your written communication (like an email) with expressive, mood-setting language.

EPISODE 29

COMPETENCY: CHARACTER

Our character isn't always strong. We all need a push periodically. Likewise, we all have the ability to push others.

ACTION: PUSH

Today, use your intuition to sense someone's need for a boost, or a pep talk, and use your strength of character to help build up that of another.

EPISODE 30

COMPETENCY: CRITICAL THINKING

The key ingredient to critical thinking is objectivity. To detach the natural instinct from attachment to personal feelings or emotions.

ACTION: DETACH

Recall a time in which you, your work, or your conduct has been questioned. Detach from your defensiveness and come up with a plan to deal with things when this type of situation comes up again.

EPISODE 31

COMPETENCY: CREATIVITY

Creative thinking is required of us all the time. For each problem we encounter, we ideate possible solutions, before deciding on one course of action. Here we must engage curiosity and critical thinking competencies as well.

ACTION: IDEATE

Take a routine task in your life that could be improved. Write down each step, ideating different ways they could be done.

EPISODE 32

COMPETENCY: CURIOSITY

Curiosity should search inward as well as outward. Question your "why." Famously coined by Simon Sinek as a business concept, our *why* – is our purpose. What is yours?

ACTION: SEARCH

Let curiosity take you on an existential journey today. Ask a lot of "why's." Start with why you are using this companion guide?

EPISODE 33

COMPETENCY: CITIZENSHIP

The citizenship competency is about being a better servant to planet and people. Small acts, like giving someone a hand to hold on to, can have a large and long-lasting impact.

ACTION: HOLD

Offer a stranger or a friend your sturdy hand today. This, of course, is to be interpreted metaphorically, but the point is to show someone you may or may not know, that you care. Put yourself out there for good.

EPISODE 34

COMPETENCY: PROBLEM SOLVING

Diversity is a concept with applications ranging from financial planning to human rights. Differences need to be explored and leveraged for problem solving as well.

ACTION: DIVERSIFY

When solving a problem, seek input from a diverse group of people, including those who think differently than you.

EPISODE 35

COMPETENCY: COLLABORATION

Have you ever collaborated on the *future* of another human being? They benefit from your knowledge, and your brain rewards you for sharing it, literally releasing dopamine, serotonin and oxytocin – a happiness cocktail.

ACTION: MENTOR

Someone you know is begging to tap into your wisdom. Identify this person, and proactively share it.

EPISODE 36

COMPETENCY: COMMUNICATION

To maximize the chance for your communication to have its desired result, you must first figure out what resonates with your audience, and appeal to them at an emotional level.

ACTION: RESONATE

Think empathetically about your audience and write down words they use, in their world. Remind yourself, "this is not about me."

EPISODE 37

COMPETENCY: CHARACTER

Being a calming force in the face of adversity is a demonstration of character, but it first requires self-awareness.

ACTION: CALM

Prepare yourself mentally by writing out a list of things that rattle you. Beside each item on the list start putting in tools you can use to remain calm, like breathing, distraction, etc.

EPISODE 38

COMPETENCY: CRITICAL THINKING

Critical thinking synthesizes pros and cons; preventing us from seeing outcomes of our decisions as strictly win or lose.

ACTION: SYNTHESIZE

Write down the worst-case scenario to a decision you must make. Consider if there is any possible upside to that scenario. Realize that there can be success in failure.

EPISODE 39

COMPETENCY: CREATIVITY

If you've ever innovated an ad-hoc solution to a household problem, you have designed a prototype. Knowing this empowers you to be more resourceful.

ACTION: PROTOTYPE

Identify a pet peeve involving a product or process in your home, and think of an invention that would solve it. Sketch a picture of, or describe below, what a solution might look like.

EPISODE 40

COMPETENCY: CURIOSITY

Reward awaits those who challenge the status quo, by connecting curiosity with imagination.

ACTIVITY: CHALLENGE

Write out the steps of something you do at work, only because, for all you know, that's the way it has always been done. Tap into curiosity, challenging this complacency, and write out ways it could be improved.

EPISODE 41

COMPETENCY: CITIZENSHIP

Your sense of citizenship detaches you from the defeatist's mantra, "I can't make a difference," and replaces it with the question "if not me then who?"

ACTION: MODEL

Commit ten minutes of your day to pick up trash around your home, community or workplace. List some specific locations below.

EPISODE 42

COMPETENCY: PROBLEM SOLVING

Problem solving takes time. It means untangling a failure, to see how something went wrong. Resist the urge to rush it.

ACTIVITY: UNTANGLE

Write down in detail each and every bit of minutia trapped inside a problem you are currently facing, in order to detect how things became entangled...and how they can become untangled.

EPISODE 43

COMPETENCY: COLLABORATION

Like the framework that makes up all competencies, the collaboration competency requires that you put forth attitude as well as knowledge and skill.

ACTION: RECOGNIZE

Just as you take pride in being commended for a job well done, today you turn the tables, and publicly recognize the good work of someone else.

EPISODE 44

COMPETENCY: COMMUNICATION

We often dread written instructions, because we know inherently they are going to be confusing and time-consuming. Knowing this should compel you to simplify your own instructions to others.

ACTION: SIMPLIFY

Prepare a set of instructions to someone on how to tie a shoelace, or some other routine activity, using only three drawings, with three words under each one.

EPISODE 45

COMPETENCY: CHARACTER

Gandhi is thought to have said "You yourself, as much as anybody in the universe, deserve your love and affection." The strength of your character begins with how you feel about yourself.

ACTION: LOVE

Write down the first three words that come to mind in describing you. Then ask yourself if your choice of words demonstrates whether you are giving yourself the love that you are giving others. Consider the advice of Glennon Doyle, from her book, "Untamed": "Be careful with the stories you tell about yourself."

EPISODE 46

COMPETENCY: CRITICAL THINKING

Curiosity enhances critical thinking. When you persist in questioning why a condition exists, you often end up with the ultimate answer you are seeking.

ACTION: PERSIST

When thinking through an important decision, keep asking "why" until that question has been answered for the final time, and there is no more that needs to be known. Write this out as a string of persistent "why's" in the space below.

EPISODE 47

COMPETENCY: CREATIVITY

All innovations must be tested, an activity that wrongfully strikes fear of failure into the mind of the innovator, who must come to understand that failure is really the gateway to success.

ACTION: TEST

Build, toss, and rebuild paper airplanes until one flies more than ten feet. Pay attention to your mental reaction to those attempts which fail.

EPISODE 48

COMPETITION: CITIZENSHIP

What we put in our waste and recycle bins says a lot about our citizenship. What we keep out of the bins is equally important.

ACTION: REUSE

Go into your recycling bin and pull out a random object. Upon studying this object, think of how you might get one more use out of it. Create a practice of reusing, for instance, plastic food containers in different ways.

EPISODE 49

COMPETENCY: CURIOSITY

We don't outgrow our sense of curiosity, we just become reluctant to engage it. Maybe we fear judgement, or maybe we just don't believe inquiry is a good use of time. Hint – it is.

ACTION: INQUIRE

Of the dozens of conscious curious thoughts you have, pull one out, and actually seek to find the answer. Write it down. You might think it's the most ludicrous question, but we're not solving world problems here. We're seeing where curiosity can take us.

EPISODE 50

COMPETENCY: PROBLEM SOLVING

The first step of problem solving is to determine if there really is a problem, and if so, how important it is that a solution be developed. Problems take time to solve. Ensure the time is going to be well spent.

ACTION: RATIONALIZE

Rationalize whether problems you are trying to solve warrant the time you are spending on solving them. Choose one and write it out below.

EPISODE 51

COMPETENCY: COLLABORATION

The collaboration competency sometimes requires you to lead. You will be more effective in this role if you have a clear alignment and communication of your vision. This will rely heavily on the empathy you show toward those you want to follow your lead.

ACTION: LEAD

Write down what you want to accomplish *for* your team, rather than *with* your team. The *team* can be from work, home or your leisure activities.

EPISODE 52

COMPETENCY: COMMUNICATION

As we become more polished communicators, we fall into a communication comfort zone where we execute in the same way most of the time. Consistency is good, but predictability is not.

ACTION: SURPRISE

Communicate in unexpected ways, choosing words and messaging mediums which may be out of character. Write down these surprising words and methods below.

EPISODE 53

COMPETENCY: CHARACTER

Developing character often means getting out of your comfort zone, and trying new things. These "new things" don't have to be game-changing decisions in your life. Start small and work your way up. You are rewiring the way you feel about risk.

ACTION: DARE

Catch yourself avoiding something today, simply because it feels new or uncomfortable. Coach yourself through it, allowing your pre-frontal cortex to wrestle with your amygdala.

EPISODE 54

COMPETENCY: CRITICAL THINKING

Critical thinking is careful thinking. This means collecting the obvious information as well as catching the details everyone else overlooks.

ACTION: CATCH

Go shopping and compare the ingredients of the private label (no-name) brand of packaged food (i.e., ketchup) with a name brand. Objectively assess the *value* of any price difference. Do you truly get more from the brand name, or does it somehow generate trust that the other does not?

EPISODE 55

COMPETENCY: CREATIVITY

The "Ikea Effect" is a bias which makes us favor things we create (including ideas), over other suitable alternatives. However, creativity needs to enhance the lives of others, not your ego. Next time you are working with a team on something innovative, stay grounded in evaluating all options.

ACTION: GROUND

Ground yourself to view all ideas equally, when considering new ways to solve old problems. Reflect below on some ideas of others that you have dismissed.

EPISODE 56

COMPETENCY: CITIZENSHIP

Citizenship is your service to people and planet. Developing this competency requires you to first be self-aware enough to see your own intolerances. There is no such a thing as "mostly inclusive." You either are, or you are not.

ACTION: INCLUDE

Make a list of prejudgments you might make based upon how another person looks. Think about how others might do the same to you.

EPISODE 57

COMPETENCY: PROBLEM SOLVING

Whether you are confronting an immediate minor problem, or a slow-cooking major problem, you are required to respond in some form. Part of the solution, in fact, lies in your willingness to own the problem.

ACTION: RESPOND

Even if you cannot solve a problem quickly, it is vital you respond to it, so that those impacted know that you are on the case.

EPISODE 58

COMPETENCY: CURIOSITY

There are hidden details, which may prove useful, if you allow your curiosity to win your attention, and illuminate that which others won't bother to see.

ACTION: ILLUMINATE

Read or listen to the news today, identifying something that tweaks your curiosity, then do your own research to illuminate further details. Don't rely on your regular sources to provide the whole picture.

EPISODE 59

COMPETENCY: COLLABORATION

Collaborations work best when synergies are created, pooling the value of all, for the creation of value for all. Don't aim for efficiency, aim for synergy.

ACTION: SYNERGIZE

Solicit the goals of friends and colleagues, and compare them to yours, looking for synergistic opportunities to work together.

EPISODE 60

COMPETENCY: COMMUNICATION

The most accomplished communicators never stop working on their craft. Nor should you.

ACTION: PRACTICE

Examine responses to emails or messages you have sent, paying particular attention to those that demonstrated a disconnect in communications. Identify how you could work to minimize a similar breakdown in the future. Re-write a flawed email you have sent in the space below.

EPISODE 61

COMPETENCY: CHARACTER

Motivational mantras about the simple act of "beginning" abound. And yet, we find reasons not to do so. Your character strengthens each time you fight through those barriers.

ACTION: START

Describe something you've been putting off, and beside it write precisely the first step you need to take. Then take it. Write down what that looks like too.

EPISODE 62

COMPETENCY: CRITICAL THINKING

Our brains are incredible data processing machines, constantly updating to create a sharper sense of assessment, and strengthening our critical thinking competency.

ACTION: ASSESS

Snap out of analysis paralysis about a decision you've belaboured. Provided you have used your critical thinking, trust your brain in assessing decisions, and make one.

EPISODE 63

COMPETENCY: CREATIVITY

The creativity competency produces innovative ways of doing things. But breakthrough innovation comes when problems aren't merely solved, but emotional delight is achieved.

ACTION: DELIGHT

Perform a personal favour for a family member, friend or colleague with an extra little something you know will delight them, rather than merely solve their problem. Write out your ideas below.

EPISODE 64

COMPETENCY: CITIZENSHIP

What do you believe in? What's going on in the world that doesn't sit well? Citizenship is about coming off the sidelines and getting involved.

ACTION: STAND

Click the "Contact Us" page on the website of a goodwill movement you believe in, and get on its mailing list. Make this the first step of something for which you really want to stand up.

EPISODE 65

COMPETENCY: PROBLEM SOLVING

As you solve problems you will produce a variety of possible solutions. The third step of problem solving involves critically thinking through these options.

ACTION: EVALUATE

Evaluate the options you have carefully set aside as "maybes." Research even deeper, poll people even further. Apply the carpenter's credo: "measure twice, cut once" before making a decision.

EPISODE 66

COMPETENCY: CURIOSITY

When we hike or sight-see, we allow our curiosity to open, and new discoveries are made. What would we notice if we looked more consciously at our everyday world in the same way?

ACTION: LOOK

Pretend your next routine walk to a familiar destination is in a different city, and observe like a traveler.

EPISODE 67

COMPETENCY: COLLABORATION

More than "getting along with others," collaboration means celebrating others as well. Your victories required the help and support of others. Make *celebrating* part of why people like working with you.

ACTION: CELEBRATE

Make a list of those who were part of a personal win, then thank them.

EPISODE 68

COMPETENCY: CITIZENSHIP

We live in a time where gender and race inequities still exist. It's on all of us to make this right, and it begins with our individual and united voices. Messages of one go further when they are amplified by many.

ACTION: AMPLIFY

Authentically recognize, then amplify a valuable contribution made by a member of a different race or gender. Authenticity is critical. Make sure it's real. But also make sure it's heard.

EPISODE 69

COMPETENCY: COMMUNICATION

In his seminal book, "Influence," Robert Cialdini identifies six principles of influence including "reciprocity" – a persuasion technique grounded in our compulsion to return favours.

ACTION: PERSUADE

If you desire an action to be taken from your communication, then emphasize the value you are providing.

EPISODE 70

COMPETENCY: CRITICAL THINKING

Keeping track of important things we hear, observe or think about, is an ally to critical thinking. Unfortunately, we fail to retain many of these moments. Life feeds you wisdom. Don't lose it.

ACTION: RECORD

Develop a wisdom recording habit, whether written on paper or voiced into your phone. Write down some wise words imparted to you recently, that you really want to keep.

EPISODE 71

COMPETENCY: CHARACTER

Has the "caring concern" of others convinced you that your goals are unrealistic? The museum of un-attempted dreams is vast. But you do not have to visit it.

ACTION: DEFY

Write down a personal goal, along with the discouraging words used by others towards it. Ask yourself which matters more – your goal or their doubt. Circle or highlight which side compels you more.

EPISODE 72

COMPETENCY: CREATIVITY

The growing field of biomimicry compels us to innovate, taking cues from nature. However, you don't have to be an engineer or scientist to adopt this philosophy. You don't even need the "bio" part.

ACTION: MIMIC

Watch how other life forms survive and thrive, and mimic, either literally or metaphorically. Put in writing how what you observed could supplement your creative instincts.

EPISODE 73

COMPETENCY: PROBLEM SOLVING

It's not the decision that's frightening. It is the known and unknown consequences of the decision, which get us stuck. Nevertheless, problem solving must ultimately land on choosing something. If you have done your due diligence, you have earned the right to decide.

ACTION: UNSTICK

Write down a decision you must make. Get unstuck by breaking it down into parts.

EPISODE 74

COMPETENCY: CURIOSITY

Your imagination is an intergalactic time traveler. Sadly, one of its primary vehicles, daydreaming, is frowned upon as pointless. Your curiosity begs to differ.

ACTION: DAYDREAM

Move to the closest window, and stare outside for five consecutive minutes, capturing random thoughts in the space below.

EPISODE 75

COMPETENCY: COLLABORATION

You may feel you are being a team player by checking off tasks assigned to you, but if you're doing so while ignoring the emotional needs of others, you are not collaborating.

ACTION: LIFT

When you notice others shutting down, check in with them. Your concern will lift them.

EPISODE 76

COMPETENCY: COMMUNICATION

Strengthening communication is as much about what you don't say, as it is about what you do say. You are responsible for what you put out to, and keep out of, the universe.

ACTION: FILTER

Revisit an email or text you have recently sent, and edit it below in a way it could have been filtered.

EPISODE 77

COMPETENCY: CHARACTER

What do those who overcome the worst situations have that those who wallow in self-pity do not? Hope. Like all matters of character building, power must come from within. You have reason to be hopeful, even when you feel hopeless.

ACTION: HOPE

Write down all the reasons you have to be hopeful about the next few days.

EPISODE 78

COMPETENCY: CRITICAL THINKING

Critical thinking is most effectively done methodically and slowly. However, unexpected circumstances require quick pivots. Large-scale sudden changes may be rare, but we get tossed random curve balls every day. Being prepared to think quickly and clearly is vital.

ACTION: PIVOT

Recall a recent pivot you have had to make, and evaluate the amount of critical thinking you gave it. Write down one thing you wish you had done, or thought, differently.

EPISODE 79

COMPETENCY: CREATIVITY

Plato is thought to have said "necessity is the mother of invention," but he lived in a time where there was still a lot of inventing to do. Nevertheless, if you think all the good ones are taken, think again.

ACTION: INVENT

Write, or draw, the craziest business or product idea you have invented in your head. If you're feeling particularly brave, show it to someone.

EPISODE 80

COMPETENCY: CITIZENSHIP

An ancient Chinese proverb reads, "Much distress regenerates a nation." Crises should bring us together. There is someone you know who could use your comfort in the wake of a personal loss. A perfect opportunity to practice your citizenship.

ACTION: COMFORT

Think of a person to whom you can reach out and just offer your ear. Offer to take on a task that could help them focus on dealing with their crisis.

EPISODE 81

COMPETENCY: PROBLEM SOLVING

Where there is a problem, there is uncertainty. Given time to fester, uncertainty will certainly do so.

ACTION: REASSURE

If you have any influence in a problematic situation, let the person(s) impacted know that you are aware of the problem, and are working to resolve it.

EPISODE 82

COMPETENCY: CREATIVITY

Creativity starts as a process with a known current state and a desired end state. But the path is never straight. Effective innovators accept changes of plans, and flex accordingly.

ACTION: FLEX

Identify an immoveable object in your path, and seek ways to flex around it. Draw out the object and write the words that help you flex.

EPISODE 83

COMPETENCY: COLLABORATION

We think of collaboration as working together, creating synergies, and leveraging complementary strengths. Sometimes, however, collaborations lose sight of why they began.

ACTION: CARE

If you feel your collaboration has lost its way, write down what you cared about that made you want to be involved with others in the first place. Discuss with your co-collaborators.

EPISODE 84

COMPETENCY: CHARACTER

Your character is being defined every day, as opportunities appear for you to swoop into action…or not. Be ready to deploy and build strong character. Swooping in to serve happens randomly. Be on alert.

ACTIVITY: SWOOP

Write out a random scenario, which could occur today, allowing an opportunity for you to swoop. Think of how your character would be used to help you out.

EPISODE 85

COMPETENCY: CURIOSITY

Curiosity is fully engaged in children, who jump in without fear of judgement. Ironically, as we grow older, we access curiosity less, despite needing it more.

ACTION: JUMP

Write out a list of hobbies or leisure activities you have put off for months or years. Then commit to doing one. Take twenty minutes today and devote time to it.

EPISODE 86

COMPETENCY: CRITICAL THINKING

Your critical thinking exists to see truth, when your own biases mess with you. On one hand, these "heuristics," or shortcuts, are key to your survival, but intrusive to critical thinking on the other. Think about how you are thinking.

ACTIVITY: THINK

Look up the meaning of *confirmation* and *availability biases*, and write out how they've impaired your thinking in a specific situation, and steps you can take to change this pattern.

EPISODE 87

COMPETENCY: CREATIVITY

We were all born *makers*, who have within us a resourcefulness to make innovative things with scant ingredients or components.

ACTION: MAKE

Go to a junk drawer and pull out an object. Write what it is below, and list a minimum of five different uses for it.

EPISODE 88

COMPETENCY: CITIZENSHIP

Showing gratitude for acts of citizenship is as important as practicing citizenship. Not-for-profits don't operate to receive kudos, but your offering of recognition provides much needed morale.

ACTIVITY: THANK

Jump on to a social media feed of your favorite non-profit, and post a minimum twenty word "thank-you" comment beneath one of its posts.

EPISODE 89

COMPETENCY: PROBLEM SOLVING

Our challenge with problem solving is our instinctive reaction to a symptom, rather than taking the time to get to its root.

ACTION: DIAGNOSE

Write down an interpersonal problem going on in your life, and how you know it's a problem. Then trace it back to its origin.

EPISODE 90

COMPETENCY: COMMUNICATION

Communication is a competency usually viewed in the context of two or more people. But you must also communicate with yourself. Treat yourself as though you were checking in on a friend.

ACTION: CHECK

Ask yourself, with intention, "How are you doing today?" Write out the words which flow below.

EPISODE 91

COMPETENCY: COLLABORATION

You will be called upon to collaborate due to specific skills and experience, but your collaboration competency will also draw upon your emotional intelligence, and ability to motivate.

ACTION: MOTIVATE

List names of three people with whom you work, along with what you know to be their values. Begin motivating from there.

EPISODE 92

COMPETENCY: CHARACTER

Sometimes character-building comes from being revitalized by what you give up, rather than what you are striving to get.

ACTION: REVITALIZE

Make a list of things you are willing to give up in exchange for achieving your goal. Challenge yourself to make your list longer.

EPISODE 93

COMPETENCY: CURIOSITY

Curiosity requires stimulation, but it has to come from inside. You will be tempted today by mindless activities, while truly valuable life learning waits in the wings. Resist the mindless. Venture into the unknown.

ACTION: SPONGE

Write down a topic of interest below and commit to becoming a sponge to learning about it, rather than straying to easy distraction.

EPISODE 94

COMPETENCY: CRITICAL THINKING

Outside pressure can lead to wildly irrational thinking, creating a mismatch between problem and solution. The word *examine* is Latin, meaning to weigh and test. Use it literally to find the truth.

ACTION: EXAMINE

Describe a complicated situation in which you are currently involved, and examine possible outcomes to the various ways you might deal with it.

EPISODE 95

COMPETENCY: CREATIVITY

You may think, "I'm not the creative type." However, not only do you possess creativity, it is your responsibility to stimulate and use it. This can often occur from a conscious shift of focus.

ACTIVITY: SHIFT

Shift your focus from self, to the needs of someone else, and list ways to be of assistance to someone in your life going through some difficulty.

EPISODE 96

COMPETENCY: CITIZENSHIP

There is strength in numbers. Citizenship requires people to come together to move the needle in some small positive way together.

ACTION: UNITE

Make a list of friends and co-workers, who are active in the community, and commit to learning more about what they are doing, and how you can help.

EPISODE 97

COMPETENCY: PROBLEM SOLVING

The problem solving competency relies crucially on organization. The way in which you organize your thoughts will assist you and others in your search for solutions.

ACTION: ORGANIZE

Break down a problematic situation into broad categories. Start with positives and negatives; urgent and non-urgent matters. Eliminate extraneous thoughts.

EPISODE 98

COMPETENCY: COMMUNICATION

In his book, "Alchemy," Rory Sutherland asserts some of the most effective communication techniques result from subtle signals rather than noisy claims. Be strategic and clever while quietly proving the value of your idea, product or service.

ACTION: SIGNAL

Describe below an activity you can *do* to demonstrate the efficacy of your idea, rather than attempting to convince with words.

EPISODE 99

COMPETENCY: COLLABORATION

People collaborate for a variety of reasons, the most fundamental of which is shared values. Revisiting this intersection is important.

ACTION: INTERSECT

Draw a large "x" below, and label the intersection with words, describing values which drew you to a collaboration. Reflect and research as to the ongoing presence of those today.

EPISODE 100

COMPETENCY: CHARACTER

In "Man's Search for Meaning," Victor Frankl asserts there can be no higher source of will, than to figure out and follow our purpose. His search became his will, and his will became his search. Are you ready to apply this concept personally?

ACTION: WILL

Write down the source of your will, as if you were to face a personal life-changing crisis. Ask yourself how/if it would help you determine the meaning of *your* life.

EPISODE 101

COMPETENCY: CURIOSITY

We observe the joy curiosity brings children at Christmas time as they shake gifts, imagining what's inside. In this way we can see how curiosity is even more satisfying when it is prolonged.

ACTION: INTENSIFY

Pull a fiction novel off the shelf at your library or bookstore, and read the last sentence. Glance back at the cover. Let your imagination take it from there. Write below, a possible storyline for the book.

EPISODE 102

COMPETENCY: CRITICAL THINKING

Sorting through available information for the truth can make our head hurt. But sort it we must, through the scrap heap of lies, biases, and noise, to get the truth.

ACTION: SORT

Compare the way the same news story is reported between two media outlets, and write out the differences below. Where do you come out in determining the truth?

EPISODE 103

COMPETENCY: CREATIVITY

Humans value predictability because it allows us to plan. But history tells us not only that change is inevitable, but also that we can adapt.

ACTION: ADAPT

Reflect and write about how you have had to adapt to change in your life. Read over your story and realize how you can draw from this experience for an upcoming situation that you will have to confront.

EPISODE 104

COMPETENCY: CITIZENSHIP

Rallying is not just for coaches during half-time pep talks, it is something our citizenship calls us to do when we possess just one more stitch of stamina than anyone else.

ACTION: RALLY

What can you do to breathe life back into a cause, which you believe in, but one that is faltering?

EPISODE 105

COMPETENCY: PROBLEM SOLVING

Wisdom is not reserved for gurus on mountain tops. It is something you possess, and can draw from. Your life is a quilt-work of failures and triumphs, and a bounty of problem solving lessons.

ACTION: REVIEW

Describe a problem you are working through now, and review situations from your past to gain wisdom.

EPISODE 106

COMPETENCY: COMMUNICATION

One of the golden rules of communication is to know your audience, because each audience is unique. But there are commonalities with every audience, such as the right to be treated with dignity.

ACTION: DIGNIFY

Craft a message to a friend or colleague today paying particular attention to their sense of pride.

EPISODE 107

COMPETENCY: COLLABORATION

You collaborate with the world around you every day; giving and taking, contributing and withdrawing. Eventually what you get out of collaboration will be predicated on the intention of your deposits. To *intentivize*, then, is to act out of a greater intention to serve.

ACTION: INTENTIVIZE

Describe an important action or decision you must face today. Below it, write out both the selfish, and selfless reasons for doing so. If there are more of the former than the latter, you must recalibrate your intention.

EPISODE 108

COMPETENCY: CHARACTER

Doing the right thing is one of the guiding principles of character. Doing it quietly, without drawing attention to it, guides you closer to altruism. To be altruistic is to be self*less* – perhaps the greatest measure of character.

ACTION: QUIET

Perform an act of goodwill silently and anonymously. Write it only in the space below and tell no one.

EPISODE 109

COMPETENCY: CURIOSITY

The acute curiosity of dogs, whose sense of smell, baited only by a fleeting and faint scent, is the kind of curiosity to which we should all aspire. We need to stop and smell everything (including the roses) with a little more curiosity.

ACTION: SNIFF

Discover something today using your sense of smell, and let your curiosity hold your attention to it. Describe the aroma, how it made you feel, and how it made you act. Time permitting, locate its source.

EPISODE 110

COMPETENCY: CRITICAL THINKING

Critical thinking requires critical collecting of opinions and views, as well as facts and figures. It is both a private and a public activity. Use it to seek different perspectives.

ACTIVITY: BRAINSTORM

Create a list of two or more people with whom to brainstorm on a subject needing your attention. Approach them with genuine interest as to how you would appreciate their perspective.

EPISODE 111

COMPETENCY: CREATIVITY

You have been an innovator your whole life. Whether spicing up a recipe, or taking the scenic route, your list of improvisations is vast. Know that you have this competency within you.

ACTION: IMPROVISE

Take a set of instructions you follow routinely to perform a task. Add, delete, modify, or re-sequence the steps to seek a more efficient and/or enjoyable process.

EPISODE 112

COMPETENCY: CITIZENSHIP

Citizenship often requires that we set new precedents. That we change patterns, or break the cycle, when we seek a better way. As such we precede, forming a new path for others to follow.

ACTION: PRECEDE

Write down a single first step you can take in a direction that makes the world better. While you're at it, do this also for a neglected part of your own life. Share this new precedent with someone you know.

EPISODE 113

COMPETENCY: PROBLEM SOLVING

Much of your success in problem solving will result from steps you take to earn authority in that role, and remain relevant in it. Taking the courses and earning accreditation will provide you and others with confidence.

ACTION: ACCREDIT

Seek out courses, or start with reading books on problem solving, like Nat Greene's "Stop Guessing." Building knowledge, as you know, is an integral part of building competencies.

EPISODE 114

COMPETENCY: COMMUNICATION

"All the world's a stage and all the men and women merely players," Shakespeare wrote. But he would certainly not approve of actors merely "playing" their parts. We must embrace our moments on stage, and perform.

ACTION: PERFORM

Write down ways in which you can make your next meeting or presentation, more dramatic. List the players, describe the set, vividly foresee your actions and hear your lines.

EPISODE 115

COMPETENCY: COLLABORATION

Collaboration is recognizing one's own limitations, and delegating to others to fill in where their talents and resources punctuate the outcome favourably.

ACTION: DELEGATE

Make a list of tasks in which you are underperforming, along with a list of names of persons to whom you could delegate those tasks.

EPISODE 116

COMPETENCY: CHARACTER

Envisioning triumph, and the path toward it, challenges our character. Life is beset with surprises, to which our character must respond with both steadfast will, and adaptability.

ACTION: ENVISION

Write down a goal you had hoped to achieve by now, the reasons for its delay, and how you will still attain it.

EPISODE 117

COMPETENCY: CURIOSITY

Alchemy is curiosity's accomplice. It is an attitude of non-acceptance, and sees impossible as possible. Most importantly, it is a "why not" mindset.

ACTION: ALCHEMIZE

Consider a process, practice or routine you perform regularly, but which you have felt requires a transformation. Draw below what that would look like visually.

EPISODE 118

COMPETENCY: CRITICAL THINKING

Critical thinking relies on rationale, on the ability to explain the past, so that we can more accurately predict the future, and make the best decisions.

ACTION: REASON

Argue the reason why you should or should not proceed in a preferred direction. Consider too, the passengers you are taking with you.

EPISODE 119

COMPETENCY: CREATIVITY

The concept of minimal viable product (MVP) asserts that getting a less than perfect product to market is better than not getting it to market at all. This philosophy holds in many life applications as well.

ACTION: IMPERFECT

What can you bring to the world, which adds value, even in a less than perfect form? Plan below how to do this in the next few weeks.

EPISODE 120

COMPETENCY: CITIZENSHIP

Citizenship has no hidden agenda. BS meters are too sophisticated for us to get away with saying we're doing the right thing, if we're really not.

ACTION: GUT-CHECK

Write down your values, and cross reference them against some of the activities in which you are currently involved. Look for inconsistencies.

EPISODE 121

COMPETENCY: PROBLEM SOLVING

Problem solving must not only define the problem itself, but determine what kind of a problem it is. Niching is the process of narrowing things down to understandable and highly definable categories.

ACTION: NICHE

Describe the familiar traits of a problem you are solving, while also, the qualities which make it unique. Does it fit into a category of problems, or is it in its own unique niche? Be very specific.

EPISODE 122

COMPETENCY: COMMUNICATION

The AIDA model, is an acronym that suggests customers go through the stages of *Attention, Interest, Desire,* into *Action,* when making a purchase. Nothing in life is this easy, but over-informing and repetition, help move customers (or non-complying people) along through AIDA.

ACTION: INFORM

Write out the specific value of what you are hoping someone will adopt. Repeat it to them frequently knowing when you have said your piece sufficiently.

EPISODE 123

COMPETENCY: COLLABORATION

Collaborating requires full proactive disclosure. Clauses, caveats, or any details, which might be unwelcomed by collaboration participants, should be addressed up front. Hiding things, and not disclosing things, are the same thing.

ACTION: DISCLOSE

List relevant, important, but less flattering things about yourself, that collaborators have a right to know. Consider how the admission of this can be used to help build trust in the collaboration.

EPISODE 124

COMPETENCY: CHARACTER

We make all kinds of promises, but our character is judged, not only on whether we keep those commitments, but also whether we own them if we fail.

ACTION: OWN

Identify a commitment you have made, which you fear might fall short of expectations, and write out a culpability statement.

EPISODE 125

COMPETENCY: CURIOSITY

Routine is great for efficiency, but terrible for creativity. When ensconced in routine we become complacent, unprepared for surprises, and we fail to see beyond well-worn paths. Your curiosity is begging to break routine.

ACTION: ZAG

Describe a routine task, or process you follow, that frustrates you. Make a pledge to do it differently. If you zig, try to zag. Describe how this would work below.

EPISODE 126

COMPETENCY: CRITICAL THINKING

Critical thinking requires conceptualization, a deep and wide understanding of a concept. Think beyond the obvious. Everyone else is doing that.

ACTION: CONCEPTUALIZE

Give a label to a situation in which you are involved, writing it in the centre of the page. Scatter all related inputs and outputs, in single words around it. Start seeing all the visible and hidden parts.

EPISODE 127

COMPETENCY: CREATIVITY

Creativity is an emotional response. If you are not feeling particularly creative, perhaps you need to stimulate your range of feelings, from good to bad. Cause an emotional commotion.

ACTION: STIR

Stir up your feelings with thoughts ranging from euphoria to doom, and list those thoughts below.

EPISODE 128

COMPETENCY: CITIZENSHIP

Citizenship is a lifelong practice in a never-ending pursuit of mastery. But how do you practice citizenship? Think kindness with a deeper sense of commitment.

ACTION: BEFRIEND

Identify a person, you know as an acquaintance, who you also know needs an empathetic ear. Offer your time to befriend them. Map out your plan below.

EPISODE 129

COMPETENCY: PROBLEM SOLVING

Problem solving is not the same as productivity. Problems are qualitative – each one unique. You cannot solve problems with checklists. Those don't help in getting to the bottom of things.

ACTION: SLOW

Think of a problem you attempted to solve in a hurry, and reflect on how that pressure affected the outcome. Visualize below, but do so intentionally, not with a checklist.

EPISODE 130

COMPETENCY: COMMUNICATION

Basic communication skills are too basic. We are taught to be technical, when we need to be emotional. We are taught to communicate similarly, when we need to do so differently. As Sally Hogshead, author of the book "Fascinate," evangelizes, "It's better to be different, than to be better." Be different.

ACTION: FASCINATE

Write out a communication to someone as you would do normally. Then rewrite it with more vocabulary, feelings and emotion.

EPISODE 131

COMPETENCY: CHARACTER

One of the best ways to build your own character is to help build that of others. Your genuine praise not only uplifts another fellow human, but it makes you more human as well.

ACTION: BUILD

Identify someone in your orbit who deserves recognition, and deliver it to them. Draw below the award you would give them.

EPISODE 132

COMPETENCY: COLLABORATION

One of humankind's greatest innovations is virtualization. The possibilities of being together, despite being apart, should never be taken for granted, nor overlooked.

ACTION: VIRTUALIZE

In the space below, make a list of people to whom you owe a face to face visit, then reach out and make it happen, virtually if necessary.

EPISODE 133

COMPETENCY: CURIOSITY

When we oppose the norm, we unlock alternatives never before considered. Imagine the possibilities of that for a moment. The shackles of normalcy, and expectations to conform have been removed.

ACTION: OPPOSE

Don't go with the flow today. Don't choose something because it's popular. Choose something because it's different. Make this promise below.

EPISODE 134

COMPETENCY: CREATIVITY

Design thinking is supposed to be thinking outside of the box, but it is taught as a sequential series of boxes. True creativity requires randomness and chaos. Invite some of this into a current project or idea you're trying to develop.

ACTION: MIX

Imagine and describe how you can spur creativity by not following practicality and convention. Draw outside the lines below of a new way to solve an ongoing inefficiency in your life.

EPISODE 135

COMPETENCY: CRITICAL THINKING

Every decision people make is a solution to a problem. Therefore, detecting people problems before they occur, would be both advantageous to you, the detective, but also the lives of others.

ACTION: DETECT

As you think through a sticky situation, seek to detect the underlying needs present for all people involved.

EPISODE 136

COMPETENCY: CITIZENSHIP

Corporate citizenship is considered part of a brand's value proposition, for the same reason that it is valued in individuals. Duty calls us all sooner or later, but you cannot claim citizenship, without performing it.

ACTION: ACTIVATE

Write down ways that you can physically act out the goodwill you possess. Write down the result of your goodwill – from a donation to a board volunteer position.

EPISODE 137

COMPETENCY: PROBLEM SOLVING

Problem solving often focusses on a symptom, beyond which, we fail to explore. Reframing the problem forces us to look at it from different perspectives, helping us get to the root.

ACTION: REFRAME

Seek perspectives and opinions of others, especially those uninvolved in a problem, as they will provide a neutral perspective.

EPISODE 138

COMPETENCY: COMMUNICATION

The most effective persuasion does not feel like persuasion at all. If you seek a behaviour from someone, preface what you're offering, with what you're not offering.

ACTION: PREFACE

List any downside, or omission, to an offering or idea you wish to propose to someone. State these in a way that evokes, rather than erodes, trust.

EPISODE 139

COMPETENCY: CHARACTER

"Code 7" by Bryan Johnson, interconnects seven short stories of seven friends attending the same school. Each kid confronts adversity, and learns a life lesson, captured by symbolic words, such as, "Become." What choices do we make when the going gets tough?

ACTION: BECOME

Reflect on how adversity has shaped you. Write out, below, a short story about an adversity episode you experienced, and how you overcame it, becoming who you are today.

EPISODE 140

COMPETENCY: COLLABORATION

Collaboration means two or more people or teams working together to achieve a common goal. But the meaning is lost if it's really just parties using one another. True collaborations involve emotional investment as well.

ACTION: CHEER

Identify some aspect of a collaboration, in which you are involved, that gives you great pride. Share a positive message about this with a collaborator.

EPISODE 141

COMPETENCY: CITIZENSHIP

The origin of the quote "We make a living by what we get, but we make a life by what we give," is unclear, but this doesn't lessen its relevance. Just give.

ACTION: GIVE

What can you give, from your time, talent, or treasure to make someone's life better? If you can, list five different possibilities, then follow up on at least one of them within the next week.

EPISODE 142

COMPETENCY: CREATIVITY

Disruption is not the exclusive domain of tech, nor modernity. Elvis and the Beatles were disruptors. Henry Ford and Amelia Earhart were disruptors. Disruptors break things. Especially old ways of doing things.

ACTION: BREAK

Make a list of old ways you are in the process of breaking. If it is a blank page, you're not yet disrupting. But there's still time. Make a list of old ways you *could* break.

EPISODE 143

COMPETENCY: CRITICAL THINKING

The word *scrutiny* is Latin from *scutari*, meaning "to sort rubbish." We often feel attacked when scrutinized, but we must embrace it for what it does; makes us better.

ACTION: SCRUTINIZE

Ask a colleague or friend to be your scrutiny partner, then take turns sorting one another's rubbish.

EPISODE 144

COMPETENCY: CURIOSITY

Nothing pique's our curiosity more than sought after knowledge, a solution to a puzzle, or a mystery. These are all ways in which our own curiosity is piqued. Why then, would we not use these "curiosity activators" to draw the curiosity of others?

ACTION: PIQUE

List ways you can use curiosity activators on others to get them interested in something about which you are passionate.

EPISODE 145

COMPETENCY: PROBLEM SOLVING

The problem solving competency requires calm in the face of crisis. Nothing good happens by becoming unhinged; and those relying upon you need to see that you are in control.

ACTION: EXHALE

When chaos consumes you, pay particular attention to your breathing, ensuring you are fully exhaling, to get full benefit. List a recent incident when you dealt with chaos, and how you would do things differently next time.

EPISODE 146

COMPETENCY: COMMUNICATION

Attention is hard earned, and easily lost. The time you take to get to your point, says as much about your respect for your audience's time, as it does about your skillset.

ACTION: CONDENSE

Before hitting send on emails today, pause to respect the time of the receivers of those messages. Trim the length of those emails by at least 25 per cent.

EPISODE 147

COMPETENCY: CHARACTER

There is no more powerful character trait than trustworthiness. Gain it, maintain it, and you will succeed. But like anything else that's important in life, trust requires practice. A little less, "I'll try," and a little more, "I will."

ACTION: PROMISE

Rather than using non-committal responses, begin using commitment responses. Commit to one new activity that will benefit your career or family. Write it down and practice saying it out loud.

EPISODE 148

COMPETENCY: COLLABORATION

The trick to successful collaborations is overlapping values. Chances are you will encounter collaboration matches naturally, because you will be in similar value paths. Take advantage of these encounters.

ACTION: OVERLAP

List some of the names of people with whom you collaborate, and the values you share with each of them.

EPISODE 149

COMPETENCY: CURIOSITY

If you've ever found yourself squinting in a futile attempt to see something more clearly, you may be losing your eyesight, but you haven't lost your curiosity. Squinting literally enables enhanced vision, which can also reward our curiosity.

ACTION: SQUINT

Examine the words in the fine print of the "terms of agreement" on something you usually accept (like opt-ins to a subscription). Discover one or two words which are unfamiliar, and research what they mean.

EPISODE 150

COMPETENCY: CREATIVITY

Innovation begins with empathy, because your goal is to solve people problems. And the only way to learn about people problems is to talk with people.

ACTION: INTERVIEW

Have a conversation with someone strictly from an empathic perspective. Don't think of yourself, nor the next question. Simply listen and learn.

EPISODE 151

COMPETENCY: CRITICAL THINKING

As we weigh an important decision we are flooded with thoughts, biases, and personal experiences. Seeing through that kaleidoscope is the value of critical thinking, which allows us to extract important bits of information.

ACTION: EXTRACT

List all possible outcomes of a decision you need to make today. Write down the thoughts and biases you are carrying before making the decision. See what influences your decisions.

EPISODE 152

COMPETENCY: CITIZENSHIP

Do not make claims about your caring nature, your commitment to citizenship, unless you can readily and naturally authenticate them with your actions.

ACTION: AUTHENTICATE

Write out some additional things you can do to authenticate your belief system, both to yourself and to others. Implement one thing to boost your beliefs and believability.

EPISODE 153

COMPETENCY: PROBLEM SOLVING

There are no three sweeter words to a disgruntled customer, friend, or colleague than "I've got this" – as long as they are followed by action.

ACTION: SOLVE

Make note of a pressing immediate problem within your control, and shepherd it to its rightful solution before the end of the day.

EPISODE 154

COMPETENCY: PROBLEM SOLVING

How many problems have you left unfinished, which in turn create flares of anxiety whenever you're reminded of them. Problem solvers need quiet time to sort through and contemplate solutions.

ACTION: UNDISTRACT

Physically remove yourself from your normal workspace and go to a neutral location (a quiet park bench is recommended). Think of one problem until you can see a path to a solution. Write about it below.

EPISODE 155

COMPETENCY: CHARACTER

Stephen Covey basically wrote the book on the character competency with "The 7 Habits of Highly Effective People." In it, among the bounty of principles to live by, is a template for writing a personal mission statement.

ACTION: RESOLVE

Write down something you promise to be, in the form of a personal mission statement, for the next 6 months. Feel free to search up Covey's template online.

EPISODE 156

COMPETENCY: COLLABORATION

Collaboration removes false reciprocity because it's based upon the principle of mutuality – an equal balance of value. Each participant should get the same.

ACTION: BALANCE

Ensure that you balance what you're *receiving* with what you're *giving* as part of a collaboration. Show the balance by placing equal points on either side of the page.

EPISODE 157

COMPETENCY: CITIZENSHIP

Humanity still finds itself in constant struggle with the fundamental concepts of human rights and justice for all. Personal introspection is required to identify uniquely held personal prejudices.

ACTION: INTROSPECT

Honestly self-audit to identify any prejudices you may have held or still wrangle with to this day.

EPISODE 158

COMPETENCY: CREATIVITY

Failure is not part of the path to success. It *is* the path. Celebrate the learning, rather than obsess over error.

ACTION: FAIL

Recall a recent event which did not go as planned, and write down a valuable learning, which you can integrate into your next attempt.

EPISODE 159

COMPETENCY: CRITICAL THINKING

Critical thinking requires a gathering of sufficient facts and points of view, then interpreting a clear and balanced understanding of what exists. Left to our own views, we defeat the ability to think critically.

ACTION: INTERPRET

Write out opposing views of the same argument, and interpret a balanced view between the two. Think of sending each view to a friend who holds a similar belief system.

EPISODE 160

COMPETENCY: CURIOSITY

Prying is generally a frowned upon activity, but it's the opposite of assuming, which has its own negative aspects. We are given curiosity for many reasons, including very practical ones.

ACTION: PRY

Pry into the actual composition of an ingredient listed on a food label in your household. Call the number on the label for any needed clarification. Pry into things that matter.

EPISODE 161

COMPETENCY: COMMUNICATION

In advertising there are basically two key metrics: reach and frequency. Advertising understands human behaviour. We will not notice, react, or even see or hear a message the first time. It must be repeated.

ACTION: REPEAT

If a message you have sent someone still remains without a response, repeat your message with a kind reminder.

EPISODE 162

COMPETENCY: COMMUNICATION

Remember the AIDA model: *attention, interest, desire,* and *action*? There's a reason attention comes first. The rest of the model is moot without it.

ACTION: GRAB

Write out words and gestures you can use to grab attention swiftly in an important message you must deliver.

EPISODE 163

COMPETENCY: CHARACTER

The character we possess is revealed in myriad forms, ranging from jaw-dropping acts of resilience, to subtle demonstrations of honour. In a world that celebrates big personalities, honour those who quietly go about doing the right thing.

ACTION: HONOUR

Develop your own character by honouring that of another human. Describe someone with resilience that you admire. When finished, send them a copy of your writing.

EPISODE 164

COMPETENCY: COLLABORATION

Collaborations should aim for partnership principles, involving close cooperation between parties, each of whom have rights, roles and responsibilities.

ACTION: PARTNER

List the things you are looking for in a collaboration, and determine whether it feels like a partnership.

EPISODE 165

COMPETENCY: CITIZENSHIP

Some of our ignorant acts of carelessness are cumulative acts against the planet. Remember, "one person's trash is another person's treasure." Embrace this as an act of citizenship, in two ways – helping the less fortunate while minimizing your footprint.

ACTION: UPCYCLE

Make a list of household items and clothing which you will take to goodwill instead of the landfill. Ensure they're clean and functional, and refrain from abandoning them in a place where they become someone else's problem.

EPISODE 166

COMPETENCY: CREATIVITY

If you've ever seen a toddler and a puddle, you know they're virtually inseparable. You've also no doubt observed the look of horror on the parent's face, pre-jump. Creativity is messy. Be that kid.

ACTION: SPLASH

What can you experiment with today, where the mess you make is actually part of the innovation? Jump in that puddle.

EPISODE 167

COMPETENCY: CRITICAL THINKING

Research says we approach problems according to our personality, but critical thinking says we must approach them without personality.

ACTION: APPROACH

The compass of critical thinking is objectivity. Prove this ability by writing comprehensively, the two sides to a situation in which you are involved.

EPISODE 168

COMPETENCY: CURIOSITY

Tinkering has just as much to do with putting things together in your head, as with your hands. Tinkering is grounded in curiosity, never really having a fixed agenda or deadline.

ACTION: TINKER

Think of some stress-relieving projects or activities to engage your curiosity. As a warm up, play yourself in a game of tic-tac-toe below.

EPISODE 169

COMPETENCY: COMMUNICATION

The way you present yourself is a reflection of both your awareness of self, and acceptable social norms. It is the entire package of how you look, sound and carry yourself.

ACTION: PRESENT

Name a person who's made a positive impression on you and list some details explaining why.

EPISODE 170

COMPETENCY: PROBLEM SOLVING

As Dr. Joe Dispenza argues, in his book, "Becoming Supernatural," there is a connection between the heart and the brain that is grossly underestimated. Meditating can enhance that connection, leading to a clarity that can aid problem solving.

ACTION: MEDITATE

Work some amount of meditation of it into your life. Download a free app and give it a try.

EPISODE 171

COMPETENCY: CHARACTER

"Position yourself, or be positioned" warn the authors of "Play Bigger." How do you want to be seen by the world? Everyone aims to be *better*, but *unique* is what provides real distinction.

ACTION: POSITION

List talents, passions and values that make you unique. What will give you that unique position in your world?

EPISODE 172

COMPETENCY: COLLABORATION

Enter collaborations in the spirit of give, take and surrender. Give generously of your attributes. Accept graciously those of others. And surrender the notion of having total control.

ACTION: SURRENDER

Seek to relinquish control over all aspects of a collaborative project. List things you should be willing to surrender to others.

EPISODE 173

COMPETENCY: CITIZENSHIP

Citizenship is the rent we pay for an earthly existence. We must think about our time on the planet as our privilege instead of our right. As Vivienne Ming put it in her Ted Talk, "Everything you've ever hoped your life would be comes from not chasing it directly. It comes from literally making yourself a better person. That is the one thing you can do to make this a better world."

ACTION: EARN

List some activities you must improve upon to support people and planet. Do one today, no excuses.

EPISODE 174

COMPETENCY: CREATIVITY

The creativity competency is about ideating new ways of doing things that enhance lives. The process begins with bending focus from the solution, back to the problem.

ACTION: BEND

Think of a solution you've come up with for a work or household function and evaluate how well the problem has been solved. Show the success or failure in the space below.

EPISODE 175

COMPETENCY: CRITICAL THINKING

Critical thinking is a vital leadership competency. Being able to repel the onslaught of noise, and often bold positions of others is crucial to maintaining neutrality.

ACTION: REPEL

Make a list of loud opinions invading sound decision making, and decide if they must be considered or repelled.

EPISODE 176

COMPETENCY: CURIOSITY

Given the choice between a toy, and the box from which the toy was extracted, the box often wins a kid's attention. Because to them, it's not a box. It's a castle, a spaceship, or a horse.

ACTION: PLAY

Find some tangible materials in your home with which to play. No devices allowed. Draw your design in the space below.

EPISODE 177

COMPETENCY: COMMUNICATION

If you've ever been moved by a speech, or the performing arts you know what it's like to be entranced. But you needn't be a world class orator or ballet dancer to capture another human's imagination.

ACTION: ENTRANCE

Concentrate on your next communications challenge and think of words and feelings to inject into it. Write the words below and find a way to include them in your next message.

EPISODE 178

COMPETENCY: PROBLEM SOLVING

Mothers are problem solvers. They're agile, responsive and empathetic, usually all at once. They follow their natural intuition, sensing signals from children that would otherwise be missed.

ACTION: INTUIT

Write down cues you have observed from people close to you, and what these usually mean. Focus on recognizable patterns and select problems to which you can apply them.

EPISODE 179

COMPETENCY: CHARACTER

Character is not just what we bring out of ourselves, but also what we bring out in others. Seize on opportunities to lift spirits and boost confidence.

ACTION: RAISE

Think of one person who needs a lift, and write out a genuine message, stating why they should be proud of who they are. Consider sending them a note or posting it online.

EPISODE 180

COMPETENCY: COLLABORATION

Great collaborators don't merely get along. They give generously, willing to part with things valuable to them, especially their knowledge. There is no point in hording your knowledge to yourself. If you're a true collaborator – spill it.

ACTION: EDUCATE

Make plans to share your expertise one-on-one with someone in your team. Write out a set of planned activities for your training session.

EPISODE 181

COMPETENCY: CITIZENSHIP

Giving of ourselves releases oxytocin in the brain. This is why it feels good to give. Imagine the reward flush that regular volunteering would bring to your state of mind.

ACTION: VOLUNTEER

If you're not currently volunteering, begin searching for opportunities to commit a meaningful, regular shift within your community.

EPISODE 182

COMPETENCY: CREATIVITY

The creativity competency has nothing to do with your ability to write a rhyme, or draw a puppy. It's about willingness to expand beyond your comfort zone, and see what kinds of new things you can do.

ACTION: EXPAND

Devise ideas to expand your sphere and force discomfort. If nothing seems uncomfortable, decide to do something you once rejected because of a lack of time, wisdom or perspective.

EPISODE 183

COMPETENCY: CRITICAL THINKING

Critical thinking is a critical competency because sound decisions require neutrality – something that doesn't come naturally. We favour things, harbour opinions, even prejudices, which we must strive to neutralize when making important decisions.

ACTION: NEUTRALIZE

Think of a current news story and write a counter argument to *your own* opinion about it. Write out your argument in the space below.

EPISODE 184

COMPETENCY: CURIOSITY

We bereave the death of curiosity as we grow older, wondering where it went, and how we can get it back. The good news is, it's not dead. But it may be asleep.

ACTION: EXPLORE

Make a plan to leave your home, and your phone, for a device-free walk, run or bike-ride. While on your outing, experience the gifts of all of your senses. When you get home write out on this page how you felt and what you might do differently next time.

EPISODE 185

COMPETENCY: COMMUNICATION

We often communicate in disjointed information bits, leaving the receiver of our message to clean up the mess and make sense of it. Apart from the presumptuousness of this, we aren't helping ourselves either. Want results from your messages? Make them easy to understand.

ACTION: REPORT

As you sit to write an important communication today, think beginning, middle, end, with just enough detail to connect the components. Draft your main points on the page below.

EPISODE 186

COMPETENCY: PROBLEM SOLVING

Obeying process is essential to problem solving. First, identify the problem. Second, generate possible solutions. Third, evaluate and select solution. Fourth, implement. Literature varies, but the overall pattern is irrefutable.

ACTION: OBEY

Write down the steps to a problem with which you are grappling, and begin filling in the content in the space below.

EPISODE 187

COMPETENCY: CHARACTER

Character is a competency we benefit by through mental toughness, self-awareness, and humility. Strength in the latter often makes us the initial mender of fences.

ACTION: MEND

If you are in an ego stalemate with a colleague or friend, it's time to engage your character for the greater good. Reach out and offer an olive branch, or compliment them authentically. Write their response on the page below.

EPISODE 188

COMPETENCY: COLLABORATION

Collaborations are united forces of people, groups or companies, which together, are more effective than when apart. There is really no such thing as a solo artist or solopreneur. Everybody benefits from collaborations sooner or later.

ACTION: ALLY

Go back through your greatest accomplishments and list those with whom you were allied. Reach out to a few and thank them for their involvement.

EPISODE 189

COMPETENCY: CITIZENSHIP

Citizenship requires sacrifice. It means giving up something in the service of people or planet. What you are truly willing to give up, is directly proportional to the impact of your citizenship. Give time, it's more precious than money.

ACTION: SACRIFICE

Write down ways you can sacrifice your time in service of others. List out three activities you could undertake this week and describe them below.

EPISODE 190

COMPETENCY: CREATIVITY

Creativity overlaps with citizenship frequently. Every time you do-it-yourself, you keep one product on a shelf, and another out of the landfill.

ACTION: DIY

Reduce is the first of the 3 Rs (followed by *reuse* and *recycle*). Think of a creative way to stop buying something you purchase frequently in your life. Add other reductions in the space below.

EPISODE 191

COMPETENCY: CRITICAL THINKING

Debates often get heated. This is good. It indicates that opinions are held at an emotional level, where human individuality and ingenuity springs forth, and advancements are possible.

ACTION: DEBATE

Rather than asking people if they're 'OK' with a decision, ask if they feel they have been heard.

EPISODE 192

COMPETENCY: CURIOSITY

Curiosity is the gateway drug to all of its co-competencies. Creativity, collaboration, critical thinking, character, problem solving, communication and citizenship all rely upon regular rousing of curiosity.

ACTION: ROUSE

Consider a small detail in your life (like a banking fee) you typically take for granted, and spend an extra minute examining it. Determine if that small detail is adding value, or taking value away from your life.

EPISODE 193

COMPETENCY: COMMUNICATION

We should all aspire to the level of an elite customer service provider in our communication competency. If you've ever been on the phone with someone like this, you appreciate the empathy, efficiency and timeliness of this stranger on the other end. While you may not deal with customers, you do deal with people who need you to be all of these things as well.

ACTION: REPLY

Make a list below of people who are expecting to hear from you. Make a point of replying today.

EPISODE 194

COMPETENCY: PROBLEM SOLVING

Problem solving is a process beginning with identifying the problem specifically, and ultimately implementing a solution. If competence has been achieved, the solution should not only make things better, but it should also revive morale among those involved, and beyond.

ACTION: REVIVE

Write out a list of visible signs that a problem on which you've been working, has in fact been solved. Provide evidence of this below.

EPISODE 195

COMPETENCY: CHARACTER

Never assume that your name alone will embed you forever in someone's memory. Consistent communication and social proof will rank you in the minds of those who matter.

ACTION: RANK

Create a portfolio of people with whom you wish to stay relevant, and set up a plan to communicate with them regularly. Create a visual 'directory' of a few of those people in the space below, placing the most vital of those contacts in the area where the circles overlap.

EPISODE 196

COMPETENCY: COLLABORATE

While we are adaptable to communicating and collaborating virtually, there is no denying the value of face-to-face fraternization, and the need to leverage this where possible.

ACTION: FRATERNIZE

Organize a list of people with whom you owe a face-to-face visit, and begin the path towards greater collaboration with those on the list.

EPISODE 197

COMPETENCY: CITIZENSHIP

While peaceful protests and demonstrations are effective, if thou "doth protest too much" goes the Shakespeare verse from "Hamlet," thou doth raise suspicion. Or worse, indifference.

ACTION: DEMONSTRATE

Limit the scope and frequency of your demonstrations. Force yourself to get into the real reasons for your protest in the space below. Be sure these are measured reasons; you gain little from overdoing it.

EPISODE 198

COMPETENCY: CREATIVITY

There is the power in tangibility; in things of substance. Ideas and actions are intangible, but they can be *'tangibilized'* by adding physical, visual symbols or signs which give them meaning.

ACTION: TANGIBILIZE

Write an idea that you'd like to share, but then add a plan on how you could demonstrate visually how it works.

EPISODE 199

COMPETENCY: CRITICAL THINKING

Logic is the casualty of rushed judgement. Thus, our need for speed flies in the face of deductive reasoning. And yet it is that very process that takes time. You cannot "click" critical thinking.

ACTION: DEDUCE

Set aside ample time to deduce reasoning and fact into a logical conclusion. Make the page below your space for logic – can you find anywhere in your life where you are illogical?

EPISODE 200

COMPETENCY: CURIOSITY

As Tom Nichols asserted in his book, "The Death of Expertise," the best thing education can do is teach us to learn. If you feel you know enough about something, you must engage your sense of intellectual curiosity, and yearn to learn more.

ACTION: LEARN

Think about an aspect of your life in which you feel knowledgeable, then make a list of things about it, that you do not know. It should fill up the space below if you have done this correctly.

EPISODE 201

COMPETENCY: COMMUNICATION

The "chasm" in Geoffrey Moore's book, "Crossing the Chasm," refers to a gap between the first people who try new ideas, and the masses who follow. Being unique is risky, but better fall into the chasm as an original, than to fade away as a follower.

ACTION: FALL

Take risks in the way you communicate. Make your own drawing of a chasm you would like to cross below. Search up Moore's book online for the visual and more background.

EPISODE 202

COMPETENCY: PROBLEM SOLVING

People don't buy $600 shoes because they're comfortable. That purchase is satisfying a different kind of need. Solving problems of others requires you to get inside their heads, because human "behaviour" sometimes helps define problems more honestly than their words.

ACTION: MIND-READ

Observe someone with whom you interact regularly and record behaviours which reveal their needs. Be it a child or a customer, the space below should be used to record what you observe.

EPISODE 203

COMPETENCY: CHARACTER

Self-awareness and reflection are paramount to character development. A certain eagle-like perch, with nature as your backdrop and fresh air in your lungs, is the perfect setting to consciously be in this state of mind.

ACTION: PERCH

Identify your perch, your unique place, and make it your go-to for deep reflection. Draw this place, or describe things about it, on this page.

EPISODE 204

COMPETENCY: COLLABORATION

Competent collaborators consciously look for ways to make human interaction better. They read cues from those with whom they work, and pick up on behaviours, which display underlying feelings.

ACTION: DECODE

Write a list of members of a group with whom you work, and enter some corresponding signals they use (often unconsciously) which reveal their feelings. Describe what that looks like on this page.

EPISODE 205

COMPETENCY: CITIZENSHIP

We don't have to be altruists in order to be good citizens. But aiming for altruism is not an illogical aspiration. Start with thinking more self*lessly* than selfishly.

ACTION: ALTRUIZE

List some goodwill ideas you have put off because they are too expensive, time-consuming, inconvenient or otherwise interruptive to your life. Is there just one you could initiate? Think self-less.

EPISODE 206

COMPETENCY: CREATIVITY

The increasing pervasiveness of AI makes routine human skills vulnerable, while making human creativity more valuable. Creative thinking is a refusal to accept that there is no room for improvement. Think in this way, and watch your value grow.

ACTION: REFUSE

Describe a process you follow simply because "that's how people do it," even though you think there's a better way. Describe that better way and contemplate what would be required to move it forward.

EPISODE 207

COMPETENCY: CRITICAL THINKING

Every action you take leaves another action untaken. Critical thinking produces choices of actions, directions, decisions and so on. You must then exercise further critical thinking, selecting one over the others.

ACTION: UNTAKE

Write down the carefully considered and probable outcomes of choices on which you decided not to take. Good and bad. What are you relieved to have avoided? What do you regret missing out on?

EPISODE 208

COMPETENCY: CURIOSITY

In "Atomic Habits" James Clear argues that changing even the smallest behaviours can lead to huge positive changes. But you have to be curious enough to seek the motivation of your behaviours.

ACTION: ALERT

Jot down a bad habit of yours, along with a few words as to why you have it. Look up the "Atomic Habits" book and look over the process – describe how similar or different it is than how you approached it on this page.

EPISODE 209

COMPETENCY: COMMUNICATION

It is selfish to hide behind modesty when you have something important to say. You may hate public speaking, or fear judgement of your words, but if it's important, you must redirect from your fear demotivation, toward your generosity motivation. D'vorah Lanksy, of "Share Your Brilliance," puts it bluntly. "You're being selfish by holding it back."

ACTION: REDIRECT

Write an important message you've withheld, and redirect your focus on those who'd benefit by hearing it. If you're feeling particularly brave, post it on social media.

EPISODE 210

COMPETENCY: PROBLEM SOLVING

Problem solving begins with recognizing that a problem exists at all. Developing this competency requires a conscious effort in noticing the cues in your environment that something isn't working.

ACTION: CUE

Write out recent signals you've picked up by paying close attention to society, culture, economics, the legal system and technology. Space them out below and make a choice to act on at least one area.

EPISODE 211

COMPETENCY: CHARACTER

Independent choice is in us all, but we overlook it constantly. We aren't defined by what happens to us, but what we do with what happens to us. This is a matter of choice.

ACTION: CHOOSE

List possessions and achievements you had hoped to have earned, along with the reasons you feel you have yet to own or achieve them. Choose one, and draw a path backwards to a decision you made. Then draw a path forward to where you achieve this elusive goal. The beginning and end is always of *your* choosing.

EPISODE 212

COMPETENCY: COLLABORATION

Collaboration requires an unflinching "what's good for the group is good for its members" mentality. You must be willing to represent your partners with equal enthusiasm as you do yourself.

ACTION: REPRESENT

When tempted to promote yourself in a group environment today, stop and represent someone else instead. Write out how it will go in the space below.

EPISODE 213

COMPETENCY: CITIZENSHIP

Citizenship reminds us to align our behaviour with the betterment of our planet. Remember that the enhancements you offer outward, can only be delivered if *you*, and the way you live, are also sustainable.

ACTION: ENHANCE

Seek ways of enhancing your own life. Make up categories like physical health, mental health, time management, fun, etc. Prioritize and begin enhancing your life, so that you can further enhance the world.

EPISODE 214

COMPETENCY: CREATIVITY

Just because innovation has happened, does not mean we stop noticing needs for further innovation. Innovation is a loop, not a line. Each new one eventually circles back, introducing a new need.

ACTION: NOTICE

What glitches have you noticed about new ideas, procedures or processes you've recently introduced, especially those affecting others? List and describe them below.

EPISODE 215

COMPETENCY: CRITICAL THINKING

When making decisions or assessing situations, we are ultimately forced to develop and evaluate options. Critical thinking dictates that we invest time to make careful calculations in reality, rather than online searches.

ACTION: MEASURE

Describe a situation in which you could think more critically, drawing from the physical world. Write down your thoughts on this below – and don't be tempted to search it online.

EPISODE 216

COMPETENCY: CITIZENSHIP

In a world that has never felt more divided, the onus is on us as individuals to repel the narrative that we must take a side. Humanity has never advanced through division. If you cannot understand someone else's views, it is time to switch on empathy.

ACTION: EMBRACE

Identify a person with an opinion which differs from your own, and embrace the opportunity to hear them out. Draft an email to that person below, and take the step to send it once you have found that proper embrace.

EPISODE 217

COMPETENCY: COMMUNICATION

Persuasive communication is its own unique craft, involving strategy, empathy, an obsession with human behaviour, and a willingness to "woo." But if you wish to woo someone toward yourself, your product, or your idea, you need to make it clear what's in it for them.

ACTION: WOO

Practice using different combinations of words, gestures, non-verbal signals that show your genuine interest in earning the favour of someone else.

EPISODE 218

COMPETENCY: PROBLEM SOLVING

The concept of scope is vital in problem solving. It demarcates that which will be left alone, from that which will be dealt with in solving a problem.

ACTION: DEMARCATE

In working through a problem, draw a line around items and issues which will be included, and keep everything else out. Show this work below.

EPISODE 219

COMPETENCY: CHARACTER

All of us are prone to moral compromise, especially when no one is watching, or when we white-lie our way out of awkward situations. Never assume that these character indiscretions have no lasting impact outwardly, nor inwardly.

ACTION: CONDUCT

List ways in which you are still developing your character, through moral struggles you continue to have. Pick one struggle and break it apart below – can you change your conduct and thus your character?

EPISODE 220

COMPETENCY: COLLABORATION

You are involved in a collaboration because of the strengths you offer, but are you putting forth the energy in giving the group everything of which you are capable.

ACTION: INVOLVE

List the things you do within a group, and reflect on whether you are being used to your full potential. It is up to you to change this.

EPISODE 221

COMPETENCY: CREATIVITY

The creative process produces an ideation stage, where open mindedness and input from all involved is required, and bouncing of ideas freely occurs without judgement.

ACTION: BOUNCE

Consider ideas you have both contributed to and heard of, during a recent brainstorming session and describe your level of acceptance of ideas of others. Write out what you can do about these ideas moving forward.

EPISODE 222

COMPETENCY: CURIOSITY

Human beings prefer routines. Routines are efficient, productive, and predictable. But reliance upon routines quashes curiosity, leaving us wandering around zombie-like, when routines are broken.

ACTION: UNLEARN

Catch yourself where you go along with an idea simply because "that's the way it's always been done," then unlearn it so that you can consider a new approach. Draw out the steps of this new approach on the page below.

EPISODE 223

COMPETENCY: CRITICAL THINKING

Deliberations in courts of law can take weeks, as jurors argue all angles before reaching a verdict. You must do the same in really critically thinking through complex situations in your life.

ACTION: DELIBERATE

Describe a situation requiring multiple different viewpoints, and give them all sufficient attention, in order render a verdict. Now consider if that verdict was appropriate to the information you provided.

EPISODE 224

COMPETENCY: CITIZENSHIP

Citizenship is all about putting the greater good ahead of your own. At the very least this means absorbing minor inconveniences and annoyances. Nobody is above the law, and putting what's good for you ahead of what's good for everyone else is both selfish and destructive.

ACTION: COMPLY

List some activities you, or others, demonstrate which bend compliance with generally accepted societal principles.

EPISODE 225

COMPETENCY: COMMUNICATION

If you have ever finished reading, viewing or hearing something and felt legitimately smarter, you have been enlightened. You possess the power to enlighten others as well.

ACTION: ENLIGHTEN

Whether you are communicating to inform or persuade, strive to leave your audience more enlightened than they were. Choose a book you read or program you watched recently that made you more enlightened and describe below how that happened.

EPISODE 226

COMPETENCY: PROBLEM SOLVING

Having an accountability partnership is intensive collaboration, but also an effective tool for problem solving. It's easy (while not advisable) to feel like a failure to yourself, but more difficult to admit failure to others.

ACTION: ACCOUNT

Make a list of possible accountability partners with whom you could establish a mutually beneficial collaboration. Reach out to one of them to help keep you in check, and do the same for them.

EPISODE 227

COMPETENCY: CHARACTER

In "The Body Keeps the Score," author Bessel Vander Kolk asserts trauma is forever embedded in our brains, and the only way to free ourselves from its enslavement is to acknowledge it as part of our journey. Just as you hold on to your achievements, in the form of awards, degrees, trophies, and so on, you must get comfortable with wearing your wounds as well.

ACTION: REBOUND

Describe an event that continues to trouble you, and reflect on whether you've ignored it, or kept it hidden.

EPISODE 228

COMPETENCY: COLLABORATION

Collaborations conjure up feelings of goodwill and cooperation. However, the truth is collaborations are bound to have turbulence, because no two humans are exactly alike.

ACTION: AGREE

Make a concession in one of your collaborations, believing that true collaborations create mutual benefit in the long run. Describe how you can benefit from making this concession.

EPISODE 229

COMPETENCY: CREATIVITY

Empathy is the first step to design thinking. If you are committed to empathy, you learn to anticipate the needs of people, often before they even know they have them.

ACTION: ANTICIPATE

Practice empathic understanding of those close to you, by anticipating their requests before they are asked of you. Plan out ways you can be more anticipatory, observing mood, body language, etc, in the space below.

EPISODE 230

COMPETENCY: CURIOSITY

Greek philosopher Plutarch said: "The mind is not a vessel to be filled, but a fire to be kindled." Your curiosity has become lazy in an era of video streaming and social media. Like a flamed-out pilot light, it requires reignition.

ACTION: KINDLE

Browse through the latest best-seller list, or talk to friends about book recommendations, to help stoke your curiosity. Write down a list of books below that would be potential books to read and share.

EPISODE 231

COMPETENCY: CRITICAL THINKING

Your effectiveness in sorting through complex issues is predicated upon your critical thinking competency which, in turn, rests upon your ability to shut out noise and distraction, and to focus.

ACTION: FOCUS

Identify convenient quiet places you can go to remove yourself from physical distraction. Take this book with you and write down your thoughts on a particular topic with which you are currently grappling.

EPISODE 232

COMPETENCY: CITIZENSHIP

Humans are motivated more by power than money. Whether it's a big company, or a schoolyard bully craving power, we must step in, when we can, with actions or words to defend the powerless.

ACTION: DEFEND

Think about either a person, or a cause, which needs a voice, then step in to do so. Write out your defense plan below.

EPISODE 233

COMPETENCY: COMMUNICATION

Expression is the essence of communication. It is vibrant language filled with colour and emotion. Important messages shouldn't be left to a mere mashup of hastily assembled words.

ACTION: EXPRESS

Recall something you have read recently that moved you emotionally. Locate it and write a passage that connected with you. Do your best to add visuals to your analysis below.

EPISODE 234

COMPETENCY: PROBLEM SOLVING

We find it difficult to decouple ourselves even from service providers which serve us no benefit. Some in fact, might even cause us harm, depleting us of resources we need for other things. But we remain coupled because breaking away introduces uncertainty, even in the slightest of ways.

ACTION: DECOUPLE

Write down the pros and cons of maintaining a transactional relationship with a service provider now under scrutiny. Contact the service provider to inquire about cancelling. Warning, they'll make decoupling difficult.

EPISODE 235

COMPETENCY: CHARACTER

As Stephen Covey insists in "The 7 Habits of Highly Effective People," we fail to do important work if we do not perceive it as urgent. But if important work is never done, that negligence will itself produce urgency.

ACTION: RESIST

Resist impulses which draw you away from important work. List three essential tasks you have been meaning to do but have always been putting off. Set dates for their completion.

EPISODE 236

COMPETENCY: COLLABORATION

Bees transfer pollen from one plant to another, so that a new plant can grow. We need to see our work within collaborations, more like pollination, and generously spread our talents throughout the collaboration's ecosystem.

ACTION: POLLINATE

Are you sharing all you have to share in collaborations? List more things you could do, and make a change to one situation in your life. Track the changes in the collaboration once you have done so.

EPISODE 237

COMPETENCY: CREATIVITY

When you realize that your social media feeds are being populated by advertisements from companies, whose websites you have visited, you have been *retargeted*. Advertising finds us, no matter how much we feel we can hide from it. Want your ideas heard? Think like an advertiser.

ACTION: RETARGET

If you've had an idea rejected, think like an advertiser, and try reaching your prospect through a different opening. Write the copy, and medium used, for that 'ad' below. Note, this works in one-on-one scenarios too.

COMPETENCY: CURIOSITY

Critical thinking and creativity will engage curiosity. That curiosity will beckon you down no end of paths, some of which will most certainly waste time. But you won't know that until you get there.

ACTION: DIVE

Make a list of some rabbit holes you've wanted to dive down, and commit to going down one. Draw an actual hole below and what you think the varying levels look like, the deeper you go.

EPISODE 239

COMPETENCY: CRITICAL THINKING

Critical thinking means deconstructing possible scenarios, clarifying what they may look like, and then making informed decisions. Even, and especially in uncertain times, stakeholders will require clear direction.

ACTION: CLARIFY

Make sure you are clear in your understanding of what you've processed, before sharing it with others. Draft up an email towards a decision that you have yet to make. Have someone else check it for clarity.

EPISODE 240

COMPETENCY: CITIZENSHIP

Altruism acts upon the interest of others, period. When we offer our goodwill in exchange for attention, we are not being altruistic. Being recognized for good work is fine, but the halo shines a little brighter when you don't seek it.

ACTION: QUELL

Plan and carry out something selfless, but quell your temptation to talk about it. Figure out and commit to ensuring no one finds out about this act.

EPISODE 241

COMPETENCY: COMMUNICATION

How effective are you at having your message understood exactly as desired? Technology is a wonderful thing, but it's made us lazy communicators. Like an auto-filled Linkedin message, we take shortcuts, resulting in unclear or disingenuous messages.

ACTION: ARTICULATE

Review your written communications before hitting the send button. Ask "Is there any way in which this message could be misinterpreted?" Write down those ideas in the space below.

EPISODE 242

COMPETENCY: PROBLEM SOLVING

While stoicism and contemplative problem solving are noble, we must realize we live in an accelerated world, where time matters. Use advanced technology to trim routine tasks, so that the deep thinking doesn't have to be compromised.

ACTION: AUTOMATE

Seek out resources, like apps, to assist you in saving time on the little things. Take action on trialling one of these resources and track how it's helped or hindered your problem solving.

EPISODE 243

COMPETENCY: CHARACTER

Tim Ferriss reaffirms the peril of the sunk cost fallacy in his book, "The 4 Hour Workweek." We hang on too long to things that don't work, and never will. Stubborn commitment to empty pursuits isn't only stubborn. It's hubristic. It might be time to get over yourself.

ACTION: CUT

Make a list of things to cut out of your life in the space below. Cut them and move on.

EPISODE 244

COMPETENCY: COLLABORATION

Identifying our shortcomings is essential to our growth. Equally essential, then, is recruiting people into our lives who can compensate for our weaknesses with their strengths.

ACTION: COMPENSATE

Describe a weakness you possess, which could be compensated for by someone within your collaborative group. Reach out to that someone for help in improving upon this weakness.

EPISODE 245

COMPETENCY: CREATIVITY

In their book "Fail Fast, Fail Often" Ryan Barbineaux and John Krumboltz argue that acting more, and planning less is a quicker road not only to career and business goals; but also to happiness.

ACTION: LOSE

Describe a risk your gut is telling you to take, and what you have to lose. List what can be lost, and right beside it counter with what could be gained. Really think this through. There is often *gain* in loss.

EPISODE 246

COMPETENCY: CURIOSITY

We feel we understand human behaviour enough to make accurate predictions as to how people will behave. The problem is that the more we learn about human behaviour, the less predictable it appears to be. Keep watching. Your curiosity is here to serve.

ACTION: WATCH

As inconspicuously as possible, watch another human being for several minutes, making note of their subtle behaviours and mannerisms. Write down your field notes in the space below.

EPISODE 247

COMPETENCY: CRITICAL THINKING

Critical thinking is the ability to construct logical arguments from various sources, derived mostly from historical data, or present conditions. However, our critical thinking must also grapple with all possible future consequences of decisions.

ACTION: ARGUE

Write out the basis of a decision made recently, and reflect upon whether you gave sufficient consideration to outcomes. Make a choice on whether the decision was a good one or if you would have done something differently.

EPISODE 248

COMPETENCY: CITIZENSHIP

Recent studies corroborate Darwin's assertion that what we display on our face affects our emotions. When we smile, our facial muscles contract, signaling our brain's reward system, and triggering the release of endorphins, which, in turn, makes us smile more. It's a happiness cycle.

ACTION: SMILE

Smile toward someone else today, and create your own happiness cycle. Write down how you felt. Could you feel the endorphin rush?

EPISODE 249

COMPETENCY: COMMUNICATION

Deepak Chopra calls the soul, "the confluence of meaning, context and archetypal stories," suggesting, "when you close your eyes and observe your thoughts, what you see is a product of your soul." Imagine the power of communicating from that place.

ACTION: EXPOSE

Follow Chopra's exercise described, and try writing a message from your soul. How did you feel about that vulnerability? If so inclined, share it with someone else.

EPISODE 250

COMPETENCY: PROBLEM SOLVING

There is a benefit to organizing thoughts that goes beyond personal peace of mind. Problems are messy. Reorganizing their components makes them less daunting.

ACTION: REORGANIZE

Take apart the various pieces of a problem, and reorganize them into broad categories, then sub-categories and so on. Like that huge pile of paper on your desk, somehow sorting it into meaningful categories makes the "pile problem" seem easier to solve.

EPISODE 251

COMPETENCY: CHARACTER

"People love it when you lose, they love dirty laundry" Don Henley crowed in his 80's hit. We all mess up, and wish there was a way out. There is. It's called an admission of responsibility. While it's never easy at the time, in the long run it will keep you out of the rumour mill.

ACTION: ADMIT

Write down an admission of a mistake you've made as candidly as possible. While you're at it, write down things for which you may not ever be willing to admit blame. Reconsider everything on this list.

EPISODE 252

COMPETENCY: COLLABORATION

Harmonizers keep the emotional level of collaborations upbeat, and ensure everyone's opinions are heard. But harmonizing isn't the role of one person, it's a shared responsibility. You may not consider yourself the "touchy feely" type. But you possess compassion and empathy just the same.

ACTION: HARMONIZE

List things you can do to bring positivity and lightness into a current collaboration, even if you always felt that was someone else's role.

EPISODE 253

COMPETENCY: CREATIVITY

The first two steps of design thinking are to truly understand the people (empathy) who have the problem, and specifically defining what the problem is (define). The sequence of these steps is important, but so too is total clarity.

ACTION: SPECIFY

Take a routine problem experienced at home or work, and dissect it down to its root components, then write the definition of the problem as specifically as possible.

EPISODE 254

COMPETENCY: CURIOSITY

Contrary to the notion that daydreaming is a mindless form of curiosity, your spontaneous seeking of answers to questions delivers a dopamine rush when puzzles are solved. To say nothing of extrinsic benefits your newfound knowledge presents.

ACTION: SEEK

Describe a random curiosity you have had, and spend five minutes seeking its answer. Write down three specific revelations you discovered through this process.

EPISODE 255

COMPETENCY: CRITICAL THINKING

Trauma messes with our ability to think straight, which challenges our critical thinking. We endure battle scars throughout life, which we must accept as part of us, neither causing us to yearn for whimsical days or yore, nor dreading an apocalyptic future.

ACTION: ACCEPT

Describe a personal setback which you still need to accept. Determine if the way you went about dealing with the setback had any role in why you recall it.

EPISODE 256

COMPETENCY: CITIZENSHIP

The "Giving Pledge," founded by Warren Buffet, and Bill and Melinda Gates, is a declaration by the world's richest to devote the majority of their wealth to charitable causes. But citizenship knows no class system. It's not up to a handful of uber-wealthy to plug all the holes.

ACTION: DONATE

Donate to a charity if not in money, then in time or talent. List three charitable causes, to whom you wish to donate. Write ways you could help each, but choose at least one with which to move forward.

EPISODE 257

COMPETENCY: COMMUNICATION

Those who speak up are the ones remembered. Whether it's the kid waving her hand in pre-school, or the professional in the boardroom, articulating a viewpoint with confidence, active participation in conversation counts.

ACTION: SPEAK

Make a list of situations in which you can summon your voice and speak out today. Plan out how you will do this in the space below.

EPISODE 258

COMPETENCY: PROBLEM SOLVING

Problem solving dissects the problem into its parts, but still views them as parts of a system. Think of problem solving like making a sandwich. It is a coherent system of ingredients and steps.

ACTION: SYSTEMIZE

Write the parts of a problem you're trying to solve, drawing lines connecting them to one another.

EPISODE 259

COMPETENCY: CHARACTER

Character is tested the most by negative externalities we are forced to confront. Enduring these tests isn't just a matter of soldiering through. It is also about learning from the experience.

ACTION: ENDURE

What have you had to endure over the past year, and what have you learned about yourself?

EPISODE 260

COMPETENCY: COLLABORATION

We collaborate with the world around us every day. Like merging on to a busy freeway, we are required to adjust, and likewise seek and expect adjustment from others.

ACTION: MERGE

Describe how you have merged into a group environment, and come up with ways you can adjust further to move in the same direction. Draw out this situation as if you are in an automobile merging into traffic flow, in the space below.

EPISODE 261

COMPETENCY: CREATIVITY

Sir Ken Robinson opined, "if you are not prepared to be wrong, you will never come up with anything original." Prepare for mistakes. *Author's note: Sir Ken Robinson passed during the writing of this book. I deeply wish to express my gratitude to him for his work.*

ACTION: RISK

Write out an idea you've been withholding, that you need to share, and set a date to do so. Search up Sir Ken's speech on education and listen to it in the background as you complete this task.

EPISODE 262

COMPETENCY: CURIOSITY

In order to understand the feelings of a person or persons, you must engage empathetic curiosity. And there's no better place to start, than in their soul. The good news is, with practice and patience, you can learn how to see it.

ACTION: PEER

Experiment with the adage that "the eyes are the window to the soul." Practice peering, inconspicuously and unintrusively, into the eyes of someone you know today. Recall below, what you saw.

EPISODE 263

COMPETENCY: CRITICAL THINKING

Neutrality and objective thinking are the cornerstones of critical thinking, but you must actually do something with your findings. Critical thinking is also about *critical linking*.

ACTION: LINK

Draw linkages between all the inputs to a situation, task or problem, and see how things are connected and disconnected. The visual you craft should give you the impetus to do something about that situation.

EPISODE 264

COMPETENCY: CITIZENSHIP

Behavioural economist, Daniel Kahneman told us a lot about ourselves in "Thinking Fast and Slow" including "confirmation bias" - our desire to believe things which confirm what we already believe. When we use it, we often put convenience ahead of true understanding.

ACTION: DEGENERALIZE

Write out a generalization you've made about something based on what you *want* to believe. Use critical thinking to degeneralize.

EPISODE 265

COMPETENCY: COMMUNICATION

The communication task of getting attention is an increasingly difficult feat. But adding spice to your language has the same effect as it does to bland food. Write, speak, post, comment – with accents, texture and flavour!

ACTION: SPICE

Look at messages you've written, and make a list of livelier words you'll use in the future. Reply to an email, employing this tactic, or jump on to your favorite social channel and post a comment to spice up conversation.

EPISODE 266

COMPETENCY: PROBLEM SOLVING

Problem solving requires patience and time to disassemble, examine, repair, then reassemble. Like a home repair, you'll never get good at problem solving, if you don't take the time to break the problem down.

ACTION: DISASSEMBLE

Take a close look at a tricky situation, and break it down into easier to understand parts. Put those parts into the space below and figure out how all of them together will help you with your situation.

EPISODE 267

COMPETENCY: CHARACTER

Assertive character does not have to include boisterous body language and an overpowering voice. The most visible assertiveness is expressed simply through action. It is the enemy of procrastination.

ACTION: ASSERT

Assert your will upon a project. Write down an action you'll do today to influence others. Take action by doing something tangible, and watch others follow.

EPISODE 268

COMPETENCY: COLLABORATION

By definition, a catalyst is a force that brings about change. You become part of a collaboration for many reasons, not the least of which is bringing about some positive change.

ACTION: CATALYZE

List specific actions or ideas that you can do inside a collaboration, to instigate change. Map the change you find in the space below.

EPISODE 269

COMPETENCY: CREATIVITY

Bob McKimm, a Stanford University Engineering prof developed the "30 Circle Exercise" to prove that sometimes quantity is better than quality in stimulating creativity.

ACTION: DOODLE

Set a timer to 3 minutes. Start the timer and begin doodling inside the circles below. Observe what you achieved in such a limited time.

EPISODE 270

COMPETENCY: CURIOSITY

Curiosity is a human need. We have a predisposition to gain knowledge, but we view curiosity as a resource – like time, and expend it selectively. Curiosity is bigger than a resource. It is living, and needs nourishment.

ACTION: PROBE

Recall a question you have had partially answered, but yearn to know more. Try to avoid using online resources to fill in the blanks and instead write out your thoughts based on your curiosity.

EPISODE 271

COMPETENCY: CRITICAL THINKING

Critical thinking improves our chances of getting as close to certainty as is humanly possible. But in order to achieve this, we must move beyond what is expected, and consider also what is unexpected.

ACTION: UNEXPECT

Make a list of outcomes you do not expect to happen from a decision you need to make today. Going forward, track if any of those unexpected outcomes came to be.

EPISODE 272

COMPETENCY: CITIZENSHIP

What a wasteful society we have become when one small imperfection destines a purchased consumer product to the landfill. We must do away with throwaway mentality.

ACTION: CONSUME

Identify a product you have purchased. Write out how you will fully consume it, and then how to still keep it from the landfill.

EPISODE 273

COMPETENCY: COMMUNICATION

Dale Carnegie's "How to Win Friends and Influence People," is as relevant today as when it was published in 1936, accurately noting that feeling appreciated is one of our deepest needs.

ACTION: APPRECIATE

Plan out in writing, how you can communicate your appreciation to a spouse, partner, child, friend or colleague in a meaningful, genuine way.

EPISODE 274

COMPETENCY: PROBLEM SOLVING

Solving a complex problem requires sufficient time be set aside to fully comprehend the problem. Problem solving is not a checklist. It's a science experiment.

ACTION: COMPREHEND

Write words you can use to have a difficult conversation with a family member, friend or colleague. Begin with, "I want to fully comprehend…"

EPISODE 275

COMPETENCY: CHARACTER

Change of seasons, milestones and anniversaries should inspire reflection not only on achievements made, but those who helped us reach them, and the gratitude we owe them.

ACTION: REPENT

Make a list of people to whom you owe a thank you, or just a hello, and then follow through. Jot down their reactions and your overall impression of the experience in the space below.

EPISODE 276

COMPETENCY: COLLABORATION

Linkedin is a wonderful tool to rekindle vital, even short-lived relationships we have had in our lives. You never know when you will want to collaborate with them again.

ACTION: REKINDLE

Open Linkedin, search up people with whom you have worked, and send them a brief "check in." Suggest a joint posting or write an update in your profile that includes them.

EPISODE 277

COMPETENCY: CREATIVITY

Innovations that click, are those based upon foresight of a need, that once satisfied makes everyone else say, "Why didn't I think of that?" Foreseeing future needs is fundamental to marketing, but also relationships.

ACTION: FORESEE

What have you noticed more and more people doing, talking about, or buying? Go beyond the obvious. Innovators see things others miss. List some faintly emerging trends below.

EPISODE 278

COMPETENCY: CURIOSITY

As we grow we're encouraged to find our path, stay in our lane, and don't ask too many questions. But curiosity can be your personal scout, sent off on missions to discover what could be.

ACTION: SCOUT

Name one crazy idea that your curiosity would enjoy researching further. Use the competencies you have developed to draw this idea out in the space below.

EPISODE 279

COMPETENCY: CRITICAL THINKING

When we step back from an idea we have created, or work we have done, and assess it objectively, we might find we're the only ones who like it. Validate your own ideas, the way you would those of others.

ACTION: VALIDATE

Make a list across the space below, of people who you trust to provide objective feedback on something you have completed. Write their feedback below for each person on your list.

EPISODE 280

COMPETENCY: CITIZENSHIP

We like to voice our opinions and express our feelings, but there's a time for quiet too. A purpose in keeping our opinions to ourselves and taking stock in a reflective way.

ACTION: HUSH

When you feel the urge to be heard, stop and listen to what's being said. Read through a social media posting that interests you, and simply look over the comments sections. Refrain from posting.

EPISODE 281

COMPETENCY: COMMUNICATION

A skilled communicator knows intuitively when a situation calls for detail, and when it needs to be summarized. You may know the whole story, and want to share all the delicious details. But your audience doesn't care. Your audience wants the cheat sheet.

ACTION: QUICKEN

Work on reducing your communication to as few words as possible. Think about an upcoming work-related communication that you can distill into no more than forty words. Think of your brevity as respect for your audience's time.

EPISODE 282

COMPETENCY: PROBLEM SOLVING

Problem solving produces options. Start fresh. Adjust. Make do. Abort mission. When none of the options fit, the retrofit provides yet another course of action.

ACTION: RETROFIT

Consider a shortage of resources you may currently have, which has become problematic, and identify alternative uses for other things you possess, which could do the job.

EPISODE 283

COMPETENCY: CHARACTER

The late Kenny Rogers sang "you gotta know when to hold 'em, know when to fold 'em" in "The Gambler." Our character is defined by what we discard, as much as what we hold on to.

ACTION: DISCARD

List some things in your life you are holding on to, which you'd be better off without. Write out a few of those things and what you might gain by discarding them.

EPISODE 284

COMPETENCY: COLLABORATION

In collaborations, you are a chemist involved in creating team chemistry. Don't look at your role solely as mixing in skills and experience. A constructive attitude must be infused as well.

ACTION: INFUSE

Evaluate your attitudinal influence within a group with whom you are collaborating, and provide ideas on how you could improve in the space below.

EPISODE 285

COMPETENCY: CREATIVITY

Day to day work routines require stimulation to break the monotony. Making games or contests, out of routine tasks can be a wonder drug for engagement.

ACTION: GAMIFY

Write down some ideas of how you can motivate yourself, and others, by making games or contests out of work.

EPISODE 286

COMPETENCY: CRITICAL THINKING

It is one thing to quietly accept others' views, but it is another to openly acknowledge the value in those perspectives, particularly when they differ from your own. Critical thinking is thought of as a private activity. Make it public.

ACTION: ACKNOWLEDGE

Voice your awareness and appreciation for viewpoints of others, preferably in a public form – online or offline.

EPISODE 287

COMPETENCY: CURIOSITY

Marvin Gaye said, "I think anything I do is done out of my lust for life. My curiosity and my dedication as an artist." When we lust to know more, we are engaging a primal yearning of curiosity.

ACTION: LUST

Turn a passive topic of interest into a lustful pursuit of knowledge. Buy or borrow a book in this area and begin taking notes on it in the space below.

EPISODE 288

COMPETENCY: CITIZENSHIP

We hold on to the guilt someone is feeling toward us, as a source of power, until the point at which we forgive. But forgiveness is a gift we can give to release another human from the shackles of guilt, while extricating ourselves from negativity's crippling grip.

ACTION: FORGIVE

Make note of any relationships which could be enhanced with the simple act of forgiveness. Pick one relationship and take that next step using forgiveness.

EPISODE 289

COMPETENCY: COMMUNICATION

We revel in riddles, knock-knock jokes and crossword puzzles, because we know there's a reward of dopamine the brain gives us upon solving them. This insight provides a tip to luring people with your communication.

ACTION: QUIZ

Draw in your reader with questions, words and imagery that forces them to figure out the message.

EPISODE 290

COMPETENCY: PROBLEM SOLVING

"A goal without a plan is just a wish," wrote Antoine de Saint Exupery in *The Little Prince*. We can't *will* things into happening, nor solve problems by wishing they'd go away. The first step in developing a problem solving plan is defining the problem.

ACTION: PLAN

Describe as clearly as possible, a problem you are trying to solve. Use the scientific method of inquiry to help you towards a solution.

EPISODE 291

COMPETENCY: CHARACTER

While laughing may not feel like an appropriate response to adversity, there is a case to be made for the sense of release that it provides, and the perspective it puts things into.

ACTION: LAUGH

Describe a ridiculous set of circumstances, you have backed yourself into, and permit yourself to laugh about it.

EPISODE 292

COMPETENCY: COLLABORATION

Collaborating with others involves trade-offs of time and talents. But there's an emotional involvement required as well, to ensure that meaningful connections are established.

ACTION: BRIDGE

Identify a team member with whom you feel disconnected, and think of a way to build a bridge to connect. Draw out a bridge in the space below and write the key words you will use to connect with them.

EPISODE 293

COMPETENCY: CREATIVITY

Design thinking relies on empathically viewing someone else's problem deeply enough to truly be able to define it. 'Problemizing' involves working backwards from symptoms to actual problem.

ACTION: PROBLEMIZE

Think of a person you know who complains of symptoms, but rarely states the problem. Write down how you would help them define the problem.

EPISODE 294

COMPETENCY: CURIOSITY

In his book, "An Attempt at Exhausting a Place in Paris" Georges Perec made a strong argument for curiosity, contending we focus too much on the extraordinary, when most of life happens in the "infra-ordinary."

ACTION: GATHER

Spend five minutes in a busy place, and, in the space below, record the mundane things you observe.

EPISODE 295

COMPETENCY: CRITICAL THINKING

Establishing the value of your time is an honest assessment of how much someone else needs it. Pricing is more than a business concept; it is an exercise in empathy and self-awareness. In this way it is also more about value received beyond the monetary.

ACTION: PRICE

Write out the value you feel just to receive in exchange for a favour provided to someone else. This is not to suggest that you ask for such compensation. It's about becoming comfortable in thinking about the value you offer.

EPISODE 296

COMPETENCY: CITIZENSHIP

The Netflix film, "The Social Dilemma," predicts the outcome of humanity's interaction with digital communication. It questions whether or not we have lost the power of choice to turn off our digital devices. Have we?

ACTION: UNPLUG

Spend five minutes without glancing at your phone, and write down all the thoughts that come into your head while doing so.

EPISODE 297

COMPETENCY: COMMUNICATION

Your communication intention will fail unless you first get your audience's attention. Despite 300 billion emails sent out worldwide every day, yours can still stand out by using a little intrigue.

ACTION: INTRIGUE

Identify the trigger words of the person to whom you are writing an email, and use them in the subject line. See if that trigger word is used their response.

EPISODE 298

COMPETENCY: PROBLEM SOLVING

Problem solving is not a zero sum game. Even in failure, we are brought one step closer to a solution. But we never know, until we make an attempt.

ACTION: ATTEMPT

Put your solution out into the world, accepting that failure is not a loss, but a learning. Write out your fears and expectations of your attempt in the space below.

EPISODE 299

COMPETENCY: CHARACTER

While our character is not frequently tested by having to produce super-human feats of strength, durability, or courage, we must still muster honour, integrity, patience, empathy, even humour, throughout an average day.

ACTION: MUSTER

Think of the little daily annoyances and frustrations, and write down how you can muster a little patience. This could come from distractions, your sense of humour, or just being more mindful of what others are going through.

EPISODE 300

COMPETENCY: COLLABORATION

Collaboration is not a handshake. It's a three-legged race. The collaboration competency binds you to your partners, creating an *inter*dependency, where your combined efforts create more than you could do independently.

ACTION: EXTEND

Your "part" in a collaboration is not finite. Describe how you can extend beyond expectations. Separate the page below in three groups, and determine what responsibility is yours, the other person's and for both of you.

EPISODE 301

COMPETENCY: CREATIVITY

There is a lot of merit to focus, but the creative process requires us to take our eyes off that with which we have become obsessed, to see what's going on elsewhere, including right under our noses.

ACTION: UNFOCUS

Write one word describing something consuming your attention, and around it write out all distractions, being alert to the notion that among those distractions may lie an important clue.

EPISODE 302

COMPETENCY: CURIOSITY

The connotation of snooping is one of intrusion. But the world's greatest inventors were all snoopy. We never find anything new by gazing into the familiar.

ACTION: SNOOP

List some topics, places or people of interest to you, and devote some time snooping to find out more about one of them. Don't be creepy. Respect privacy. Research what's available publicly.

EPISODE 303

COMPETENCY: CRITICAL THINKING

Keeping our reasoning uncontaminated from noise is a constant battle. But just as we must delete unwanted material from our digital devices to make space, we must also do so with our minds. Space is freedom.

ACTION: DELETE

Write out biases which have recently assaulted your critical thinking, and consciously remove them by crossing them out and adding strategies you'll use to reduce them.

EPISODE 304

COMPETENCY: CITIZENSHIP

According to Dr. Steven Stosny, in Psychology Today, self-regulation is "a behaviour to act in your long-term best interest, consistent with your deepest values."

ACTION: SELF-REGULATE

Stop to think if a decision you are making today is both good for you, as well as congruent with your values. If not, regulate your response with a few other ideas.

EPISODE 305

COMPETENCY: COMMUNICATION

One of the most powerful motivators is fear, and thus it is often used manipulatively in advertising and life. This should not discourage us, however, from innocently invoking its lure as we try to gain attention of others.

ACTION: SPOOK

Think of light-hearted ways in which you might use negative consequence to gain someone's attention. Try it out on someone you trust will give you honest feedback.

EPISODE 306

COMPETENCY: PROBLEM SOLVING

The world keeps spinning regardless of our schedules. We are passengers on a rotation around the sun, and time does not wait for us to solve problems. We must therefore clear space so that we can prioritize them.

ACTIVITY: CLEAR

Clear a space in your day to work on a specific problem. Place this book in that empty space and write down whatever comes to your mind.

EPISODE 307

COMPETENCY: CHARACTER

To object to something is not merely to disagree, it is verbally drawing a line. Your character will be tested by your willingness to object when you witness a wrong.

ACTION: OBJECT

Recall a recent injustice, of which you are aware, and write out how you can best make your objection known. Then use your voice. It has power.

EPISODE 308

COMPETENCY: COLLABORATION

Collaborations form because there is not only strength, but synergy in numbers. Together, collaborators are better equipped to battle the competition, or even just pre-existing elements or conditions.

ACTION: BATTLE

In taking on a particularly tough challenge, with whom would you feel comfortable going into battle? Write their names and qualities in the space below.

EPISODE 309

COMPETENCY: CREATIVITY

Life is uncertain. We should be elevating our creativity, as if in a state of desperation, even when things appear to be stable.

ACTION: ELEVATE

Think about, and write down how you can elevate the way you do things at work, home and in life in general.

EPISODE 310

COMPETENCY: CURIOSITY

Webster defines the verb "muck" as "engaging in aimless activity." But when activity engages the imagination, it is anything but aimless.

ACTION: MUCK

Go through your kitchen's junk drawer and discover an otherwise useless item, which could be put to some practical use. Make notes below of how your sense of curiosity was engaged in this activity.

EPISODE 311

COMPETENCY: CRITICAL THINKING

Critical thinking is as much about what is excluded, as much as what is included. Consider all sides of the story…provided they belong in the story.

ACTION: DISQUALIFY

Write down a decision you need to make, listing the important considerations, then go through those considerations one more time, disqualifying those inputs that would be better left out.

EPISODE 312

COMPETENCY: CITIZENSHIP

"You reap what you sow" is a guiding principle of life. Your sense of citizenship expands the context of this belief to include global consequences of personal conduct.

ACTION: SOW

Consider a small change in your life that would have positive impact on people or planet. Think of something you can sow today. Sow that seed.

EPISODE 313

COMPETENCY: COMMUNICATION

Hearing is a physical function, involving the reception of noises and tones as stimuli. But hearing also requires an open attitude. It is the gatekeeper for what we allow in. "There's grace in being willing to know and hear others," chimes Michelle Obama, in her book, "Becoming."

ACTION: HEAR

Circle back to a recent communication, and hear it again, in its entirety. Write down what you missed.

EPISODE 314

COMPETENCY: PROBLEM SOLVING

One of the biggest challenges in problem solving is determining the factual construct of a problem, and refuting information which could be hearsay, prejudicial, or otherwise false or misleading.

ACTION: REFUTE

List every piece of information you know about a current problem you are trying to solve. Revisit each item one at a time to determine not only factuality, but also relevance.

EPISODE 315

COMPETENCY: CHARACTER

Adversity is a part of life. You will make mistakes, and the unexpected will blow up your best laid plans, presenting daunting challenges. Survive these, and you will survive.

ACTION: SURVIVE

Write down your worst case scenario of a situation that lingers in your mind, and think not about what you would do, but how you would react mentally. How confident do you feel in your mental ability to survive a crisis?

EPISODE 316

COMPETENCY: COLLABORATION

For all of the benefits of collaboration there still exists naturally occurring human instincts to score keep and compare. When these feelings occur it is crucial to remember why you entered into a collaboration.

ACTION: REMEMBER

Take a moment to remember the values brought to the table by those with whom you collaborate. Use those values to help build a strong bond.

EPISODE 317

COMPETENCY: CREATIVITY

Some of the world's greatest inventions, like penicillin and radioactivity, were the result of lucky accidents. When creativity seems waning, flip things over to see things from a totally different viewpoint.

ACTION: FLIP

Flip a routine and discover something new. Write out a different route, or different viewpoint you'll follow today.

EPISODE 318

COMPETENCY: CURIOSITY

The Harvard Business Review reported business leaders acknowledge the power of curiosity, but at the same time refuse to operationalize it because it's not thought to be "efficient." *You* can recalibrate this imbalance by conducting simple, and even unnoticed experiments.

ACTION: EXPERIMENT

Here's a simple experiment about curiosity to get you into the mindset. Ask your colleagues today "what are you curious about?" Describe their verbal and non-verbal reactions below.

EPISODE 319

COMPETENCY: CRITICAL THINKING

Correlation is the practice of drawing relationships between two or more entities or events. But it isn't just useful to show connections, it also provides insights required for critical thinking.

ACTION: CORRELATE

Consider a relationship with another person in which tension has arisen. Work backwards, identifying events which led to the disagreement. Use your critical thinking skills to determine if there is a path to reconciliation.

EPISODE 320

COMPETENCY: CITIZENSHIP

There are two kinds of people. Those who have fallen, and those who will fall. Consoling is the act of comforting someone who has fallen. Our sense of citizenship compels us to do so.

ACTION: CONSOLE

Reach out to someone in your world who needs to hear you say the words "I'm here." Describe what you talk about and how you felt during this discussion.

EPISODE 321

COMPETENCY: COMMUNICATION

If you want the attention of another human being you must often use extraordinary measures. Counter-intuitiveness is one way of achieving this. Think of what is expected, then do/say something very unexpected.

ACTION: SHOCK

Write down the opposite of what the receiver of a message would expect to read from you. With their attention now spurred, continue until you've completed your intended message.

EPISODE 322

COMPETENCY: PROBLEM SOLVING

Hollywood's depiction of "the problem solver" is starkly different from the real-life, competent problem solver. Problem solving involves accumulating evidence, not destroying it.

ACTION: ACCUMULATE

Think of a problem in which you are currently involved, and make a list of every last shred of data you'll need to collect.

EPISODE 323

COMPETENCY: CHARACTER

Strong character means standing up for what's right, which often puts you in the minority. In this scenario, you must be prepared to sometimes walk alone.

ACTION: WALK

Recall and evaluate, your character's performance in a recent event in which you had to choose between being popular and being right. Decide if you would change anything and describe that in the space below.

EPISODE 324

COMPETENCY: COLLABORATION

Amalgamating represents a more serious mindset to collaborating, acknowledging that there is a formal commitment to becoming a united entity. Do not proceed unless you understand fully the commitment of you and your partner(s).

ACTION: AMALGAMATE

Write down a list of items to include in a frank conversation with your would-be collaborative partner(s) around expectations. Use the space below to make notes during this conversation.

EPISODE 325

COMPETENCY: CREATIVITY

Commercialization is the innovator's bet that their creation satisfies a problem shared by many. It's a coming out party for an idea! But there's always a risk of rejection, with which you must become comfortable. Otherwise you can cancel the celebration plans.

ACTION: COMMERCIALIZE

Whether you're an inventor or not, you probably withhold ideas for any number of reasons. Write down what's holding you back.

EPISODE 326

COMPETENCY: CURIOSITY

Creeping *is* creepy, if you're checking someone out on social channels with ill-intent. But if you are a career builder, entrepreneur, business developer, or all of the above, you *should* be creeping one social platform habitually.

ACTION: CREEP

Get a Linkedin account, if you don't already have one. If you're already there, find and follow people who can help you. Move beyond being creepy by sending a personalized message to connect.

EPISODE 327

COMPETENCY: CRITICAL THINKING

Fake news should hit our senses like an odorous trigger to the nasal passage, compelling us to eliminate its presence immediately.

ACTION: SEPARATE

Write down an example of fake news you have discovered, and beside it, write the counter-balancing fact.

EPISODE 328

COMPETENCY: CITIZENSHIP

Citizenship includes acceptance of all humans. It is a proclamation of inclusion. But inclusion doesn't stop at colour and gender. If it is to be all encompassing, it must also include enemies.

ACTION: OPEN

See the good in everyone, including someone you dislike. Write about this honest admission below.

EPISODE 329

COMPETENCY: COMMUNICATION

Praise is not to be doled out superficially. If you cannot praise from true feelings, then what you're actually doing is flattering. And despite its claim, it does not get you everywhere.

ACTION: PRAISE

Praise someone authentically, generously and intentionally. Plan it out so that you can be sure that it is felt.

EPISODE 330

COMPETENCY: PROBLEM SOLVING

Problem solving involves finding bugs, then debugging. You must accept that bugs aren't only inevitable, but a pathway to the solution.

ACTION: DEBUG

What are the "bugs" in a problem you are trying to solve? Remember, there is an underlying causation for all glitches.

EPISODE 331

COMPETENCY: CHARACTER

What you merit (deserve) is based upon proof of what you have earned. The first person from whom you merit recognition is yourself.

ACTION: MERIT

Write down below why you merit self-recognition. Split up into areas such as career/business, personal, family, etc.

EPISODE 332

COMPETENCY: COLLABORATION

Collaborations gain synergy from the diverse strengths of diverse people, but all participants must effect positive chemistry.

ACTION: EFFECT

Think about the dynamic of a group in which you are currently involved, and write an idea of how you can impact it in a positive way, beyond your technical skills and experience.

EPISODE 333

COMPETENCY: CREATIVITY

Creativity is not a straight line, but a series of twists and turns, failures and wins, and many surprises. Embrace unexpected turns, they may take you places you need to go.

ACTION: TURN

Extract a positive outcome of a recent turn of events. Draw a winding line in the space below and write how and when turns in the road happened.

EPISODE 334

COMPETENCY: CURIOSITY

"Freakonomics," by Steven Levitt and Stephen Dubner, was a trailblazing study of human behaviour, why it is so predictable, and why we, ironically, often predict incorrectly.

ACTION: SLICE

With a nod to the cover art of "Freakonomics," slice through a piece of fruit. Record the detail of what you observe inside. Go beyond colour and texture. Smell it. View it from all angles. Jot down your observations, and/or doodle a sketch in the space below.

EPISODE 335

COMPETENCY: CRITICAL THINKING

Critical thinking is valued because of its inherent efficiency. It saves time and allows us to make accurate predictions, but only *if* we eliminate personal biases.

ACTION: PREDICT

Recall a recent occasion in which you made an incorrect prediction about someone you thought you knew, based upon a bias held about them.

EPISODE 336

COMPETENCY: CITIZENSHIP

Citizenship is a competency burrowed inside of us all. The impact you make on the world begins with small changes you make yourself.

ACTION: IMPACT

List the personal habits you could augment slightly which would impact the world in a positive way.

EPISODE 337

COMPETENCY: COMMUNICATION

Communicating good news provides tremendous opportunity for engagement from those with whom you share it. Take advantage of this. Proclaim victories and invite everyone to celebrate.

ACTION: PROCLAIM

Review past messages in which you have shared good news to friends and colleagues. Question whether you made it a big enough deal, and plan to make the next announcement into a proclamation!

EPISODE 338

COMPETENCY: PROBLEM SOLVING

Problems take time to solve, but at a certain point, you have to get to the solving part. Hasten to a solution where "good" will work, rather than waiting for perfect.

ACTION: HASTEN

Write down a path to a decision between options on which you have evaluated to solve a problem. Use action words along the way to hasten this process.

EPISODE 339

COMPETENCY: CHARACTER

Your character is shaped by your resolve to follow through on your commitment, despite the doubt of others, or the sacrifices you must make.

ACTION: SCRAP

Write down a short or long term goal you have, and make a list of things you're willing to scrap to make it happen.

EPISODE 340

COMPETENCY: COLLABORATION

Collaborations traditionally mean sharing resources, including stamina and endurance. When exhaustion grips a member of your team, it is your role to step in.

ACTION: RELIEVE

Use empathy to understand the need of someone with whom you collaborate, and offer to take something off their plate. Describe what specific tasks you will undertake to make this happen.

EPISODE 341

COMPETENCY: CREATIVITY

Creativity is rarely about starting from scratch. It is more often about seeing something through your unique lens, then re-creating something else in your own way.

ACTION: RECREATE

Describe your creative spin on something that's been done previously, be it a routine process, or a dinner recipe.

EPISODE 342

COMPETENCY: CURIOSITY

When we wander, with no specific goal in mind, we discover things we wouldn't usually notice. Unguided wandering uncaps curiosity, possibly making the aimless quite fruitful.

ACTION: WANDER

Wander through a bookstore or library until you find a title which piques your curiosity, and pull it off the shelf for a closer peak inside. Note, this works in a virtual bookstore too. Write down a few thoughts on the book in the space below.

EPISODE 343

COMPETENCY: CRITICAL THINKING

You think critically every day, making inferences from an avalanche of information. In fact it is your very power of inference that helps you make sense of it all.

ACTION: INFER

Review a long email written to you, with a request for action on your part. Condense this message down into the 5W's only.

COMPETENCY: CITIZENSHIP

The citizenship competency is your selflessness competency. It is you putting yourself out to the world with a "free for hire" sign.

ACTION: PROACT

Write down a goodwill goal that you have been putting off, then proactively contact local organizations or chapters and offer to help. Write your 'free for hire" sign that offers this help in the space below.

EPISODE 345

COMPETENCY: COMMUNICATION

Effective communications grabs attention long enough to push a message through, which is intended to generate a desired response. But how to get that attention? Seek to mesmerize.

ACTION: MESMERIZE

Write down the name of someone to whom you must reach today, along with a list of words, expressions and symbols you know will grab their attention.

EPISODE 346

COMPETENCY: PROBLEM SOLVING

Problem solving follows the steps of: problem identification; solution alternative creation; alternative selection; and solution implementation. Don't let life's interruptions prevent you from completing each one.

ACTION: FIXATE

Write out the four steps from above, and ensure that a problem you're trying to solve is being guided through them sufficiently. Apply the steps to your specific example.

EPISODE 347

COMPETENCY: CHARACTER

Your actions, more than anything else, will be most closely associated with your personal brand. As Clifton Taulbert and Gary Schoeniger accurately claim in their brilliant book, "Who Owns the Ice House?" when you fulfill commitments, "your reputation becomes your brand."

ACTION: BRAND

Write down a list of three words you want people to associate with you, then write down specific actions you can take to validate this association.

EPISODE 348

COMPETENCY: COLLABORATION

Ironically, the most powerful act we can do is to release some of our coveted power. Collaboration is not just doing things, but also letting others do them.

ACTION: RELEASE

Make a list of all the things within your power, and identify just one which can be given to someone else.

EPISODE 349

COMPETENCY: CREATIVITY

If you have an imagination, you are creative. And since your imagination is at work all the time, you are in a constant state of creativity.

ACTION: PICTURE

You have designed hundreds of innovations in your imagination. Today catch yourself processing one of those, and sketch it out below.

EPISODE 350

COMPETENCY: CURIOSITY

What if we used hearing, smelling, touching, tasting as much as we did seeing? It makes sense to use all senses.

ACTION: SENSE

Take this book with you, along with a pen or pencil, and go sit outside for few minutes. Close your eyes, focusing on what you smell, hear, and feel. Draw or write what you experience.

EPISODE 351

COMPETENCY: CRITICAL THINKING

Critical thinking is so revered that when we have used it, we feel we can predict outcomes almost flawlessly. However, we must enter into critical thinking knowing that very few things in life are certain.

ACTION: UNPREDICT

Write down something you are certain will happen today, along with three different outcomes. Place a check beside which outcome came to be.

EPISODE 352

COMPETENCY: CITIZENSHIP

In the "The Lorax," Dr. Seuss wrote, "Unless someone like you cares a whole awful lot, nothing is going to get better. It's not." We must do less guessing; and more 'unlessing'.

ACTION: UNLESS

Brainstorm ideas how **you** can make the world cleaner and/or kinder. Involve family and friends.

EPISODE 353

COMPETENCY: COMMUNICATION

The most celebrated novelists and screenplay writers devote pages to character development, unpacking details methodically, so that audiences fully understand them.

ACTION: UNPACK

Write out some aspect of yourself, using as many words as you feel are required, to adequately unpack all the benefits you bring to your family, friends, community, job, or potential employer.

EPISODE 354

COMPETENCY: PROBLEM SOLVING

Attitude is often the key to unlocking the problem solving process. It begins with a mindset of being open to all optional solutions generated.

ACTION: UNLOCK

Reflect on a problem in which you are currently locked, and answer the question, "Am I being stubborn?" Answer the question in the positive and negative in the space below.

EPISODE 355

COMPETENCY: CHARACTER

What would happen if we could mute the voices which inhibit us. Character building requires that we *uninhibit* ourselves from fear.

ACTION: UNINHIBIT

Write down what you would really lose by proceeding with your gut on an imminent decision. Ask yourself if you can afford to lose those things.

EPISODE 356

COMPETENCY: COLLABORATION

There's an economic aspect of collaboration that views us all as collaborators within a community. The support-local movement is a case in point. Buying local, makes you an invaluable collaborator within your community, and unlimits the growth of small businesses and community economies.

ACTION: UNLIMIT

Buy something from a local vendor. Send feedback to the vendor, and if you are happy, write an online positive review.

EPISODE 357

COMPETENCY: CREATIVITY

What if you could unknow everything you know? You possessed the same capacity to create, but you had no prior knowledge about possible and impossible? You wouldn't be discouraged with failure, because you wouldn't know the feeling of failure.

ACTION: UNKNOW

Write down the "knowns," you would be better off "unknowing." Describe what you could do with your time if it were not spent worrying about unknowns.

EPISODE 358

COMPETENCY: CURIOSITY

Curiosity takes energy and effort, but given our access to information, there is no excuse for not learning something new everyday.

ACTION: UNTAP

Follow through on a random question entering your head as you commute, run, or bike. Untap curiosity. Learn something new.

EPISODE 359

COMPETENCY: CRITICAL THINKING

The universe has no emotion. It simply does not care. It does not judge. For this, it is a role model in critical thinking, from which we can learn to *unbias* ourselves.

ACTION: UNBIAS

Write down a biased thought you had today, and reflect on how it shaped a decision you made. Decide to remove that bias the next time you make a similar decision. Predict the difference between the two experiences.

EPISODE 360

COMPETENCY: CITIZENSHIP

The competency of citizenship supports the adage that it is better to give than to receive. But giving also gives back to the giver with the feel good hormone, dopamine, delivered by the brain's reward system.

ACTION: UNWRAP

Unwrap happiness for you and the recipient of your kindness. Fold this page, and inside write something kind about yourself and those with whom you are close.

EPISODE 361

COMPETENCY: COMMUNICATION

You will announce things to the world in coming months. The arrival of a baby, the engagement to a partner, a new business, a new idea. Big news requires more than announcements. It should be treated more like dramatic unveilings.

ACTION: UNVEIL

In the space below, plan how you could first "tease" a major announcement, and build toward a dramatic unveiling.

EPISODE 362

COMPETENCY: PROBLEM SOLVING

Humans screw up. And while we can't unscrew our screwups, we can learn from them, so that when similar situations arise we do not fall into the same trap.

ACTIVITY: UNSCREW

Write down a problem you are trying to solve at the moment, and ask "Have I been down this road before?" If so, describe a previous occurrence and see if you are doing anything different now.

EPISODE 363

COMPETENCY: CHARACTER

The most fundamental and powerful proof of character is standing by a pact made to yourself. *You* must earn trust in yourself as well. When circumstance and naysayers say stop to one of these personal pacts, unstop.

ACTIVITY: UNSTOP

Write down a promise you made to yourself, along with any reasons why you should stop. Seek the character required to unstop from books, old notes, or even earlier parts of this book.

EPISODE 364

COMPETENCY: COLLABORATION

Collaborations thrive until egos collide. As Ryan Holliday aptly put it in the title, and throughout his book, "Ego is the Enemy." Unload ego at the door, prior to entering a collaboration.

ACTION: UNLOAD

Ask whether your ego is curtailing the success of a collaboration of which you are a part. Decide to park your ego when entering into your next meeting with your collaborator. See the difference in what happens next.

EPISODE 365

COMPETENCY: CREATIVITY

The most limiting thing you can do for your creativity is stay only on safe and proven paths. When something isn't working, or could work better, unfollow the repeat cycle.

ACTION: UNFOLLOW

Reflect upon a part of your life on which you had hoped would be improved by now, and seek out a different path to correct its course. Choose to unfollow familiar paths by coming up with new ideas and approaches to your life.

EPISODE 366

COMPETENCY: CURIOSITY

Curiosity is the key to all human competencies. But opening its potential requires effort, and a redirect away from the way things are done. It takes undoing.

ACTION: UNDO

Reflect on ways in which your curiosity can open doors for you, and in turn, unlock ways in which you can have greater impact. It is time to undo the way things have been done.

REFERENCES

The following is a list of authors, journalists and artists whose work informed, inspired and enlightened me while producing both The Daily Undoing podcast and book. Their work is highly recommended.

Barbineaux, R., & Krumbolt, J. (2013) *Fail Fast, Fail Often: How Losing Can Help You Win.* TarcherPerigee

Bell, M. (2011, April 1). Marvin Gaye: A Wrenched Heart Resting in a Bed of Pathos. *The Washington Post.*

Carnegie, D. (1998). *How to Win Friends and Influence People.* Gallery Books

Chopra, D. (2012, May 21) The Chopra Well [Video]. YouTube. https://www.youtube.com/user/TheChopraWell

Cialdini, R. (2006) *Influence: The Psychology of Persuasion* (Revised ed.). Harper Business

Clear, J. (2018) *Atomic Habits: An Easy and Proven Way to Build Good Habits and Break Bad Ones.* Avery

Covey, S. (1989) *The 7 Habits of Highly Effective People.* Simon and Schuster

Dickens, C. (1859) *A Tale of Two Cities.*

Dispenza, J. (2017) *Becoming Supernatural: How Common People are Doing Uncommon Things.* Hay House Inc.

Dubner, S. & Levitt, S. (2005) *Freakonomics.* Harper Collins

Caprice, A. (2000) *The Expanded Quotable Einstein,* Princeton University Press

Exupery, A. (1943) *The Little Prince.*

Ferriss, T. (2007) *The 4 Hour Work Week.* (Updated ed.). Harmony

Frankl, V. (1946) *Man's Search for Meaning.*

Friedman, T. (2016) *Thank You For Being Late: An Optimists Guide to Thinking in the Age of Acceleration* Farrar, Straus and Giroux

Gino, F. (2018). The Business Case for Curiosity. *Harvard Business Review.* https://hbr.org/2018/09/the-business-case-for-curiosity

Greene, N. (2017) *Stop Guessing: The 9 Behaviors of Great Problem Solvers,* Berrett-Koehler Publishers

Henley, D. (1982) Dirty Laundry [Song]. On *I Can't Stand Still.* Asylum.

Hogshead, S. (2016) *Fascinate: How to Make Your Brand Impossible to Resist,* Harper Business

Holliday, R. (2016) *Ego is the Enemy.* Portfolio

Jacquet, L. (Director). (2005). *March of the Penguins* [Film]. National Geographic Films.

Johnson, B. (2017) *Code 7: Cracking the Code for an Epic Life.* Candy Wrapper

Kahneman, D. (2013) *Thinking Fast and Slow,* Farrar, Strauss & Giroux

King, M.L. (1963, August 28) I Have a Dream. [Speech]. Lincoln Memorial, Washington D.C.

Leslie, I. (2015) *Curious: The Desire to Know and Why Your Future Depends on it.* Basic Books

Merriam-Webster. (2020). Contemplate. In Merriam-Webster.com dictionary. https://www.merriam-webster.com/dictionary/contemplate

Merriam-Webster. (2020). Muck. In Merriam-Webster.com dictionary. https://www.merriam-webster.com/dictionary/muck

McKimm, R. (2013). Exercise: Adaptation of the 30 Circles Test. [Blog]. *Stanford University Youth Creativity, Innovation & Sustainable Leadership.* https://hbr.org/2018/09/the-business-case-for-curiosity

Moore, G. (2014) *Crossing the Chasm: Marketing and Selling Disruptive Products to Mainstream Customers* (3rd ed.). Harper Business

Nichols, T. (2017). *The Death of Expertise: The Campaign Against Established Knowledge and Why it Matters.* Oxford University Press

Perec, Georges (1975) *An Attempt at Exhausting a Place in Paris.*

Plutarch (1939) *On Curiosity.* Loeb Classical Library.

Ramadan, A., Petersen, D., Lochhead, C., Maney, K. (2016) *Play Bigger: How Pirates, Dreamers, and Innovators Create and Dominate Markets.* Harper Business

Robinson, K. (2007, January 7) Do Schools Kill Creativity? [Video]. YouTube. TedTalk https://www.youtube.com/watch?v=iG9CE55wbtY

Rogers, K. (1978) The Gambler [Song]. On *The Gambler.* United Artists.

Seuss, Dr. (2018) *The Lorax.* Penguin Random House

Shakespeare, W. (2019) *As You Like It.* Dr. B.A. Mowat & P. Werstine (eds.) Simon and Schuster (original work published 1599)

Shakespeare, W. (1604) Hamlet. Oxford Text Archive, http://hdl.handle.net/20.500.12024/1446.

Sinek, S (2011) *Start With Why: How Great Leaders Inspire Everyone to Take Action.* Portfolio

Stosny, S. (2020). Self Regulation: The Most Important Skill in Love and Life. [Blog]. *Psychology Today.* https://www.psychologytoday.com/ca/blog/anger-in-the-age-entitlement/202004/self-regulation

Sutherland, R. (2019) *Alchemy: The Dark Art and Curious Science of Creating Magic in Brands, Business, and Life* (Revised ed.). William Morrow

Taulbert, C. & Schoeniger, G. (2010) *Who Owns the Ice House? Eight Life Lessons From An Unlikely Entrepreneur.* ELI Press

Vander Kolk, B (2015) *The Body Keeps the Score: Brain, Mind, and Body in the Healing of Trauma* (Revised ed.). Penguin Books

Vaynerchuk, G. (2018) *Crushing it – How Great Entrepreneurs Build Their Business and Influence, and How You Can Too.* Harper Business

ABOUT THE AUTHOR

David Gaudet has been teaching marketing at the Southern Alberta Institute of Technology, in Calgary, AB since 2002. He is the co-author of Canada's best-selling marketing textbook, "MKTG: Principles of Marketing," and has contributed to four other textbooks in North America.

As an entrepreneur since the early 90's, David is the founder of multiple businesses ranging from marketing, marketing research, and branding to real estate, and has given countless talks at entrepreneurial, ed-tech, and leadership conferences across Canada and the United States. He is a passionate trumpeter of small businesses, and working with their founders on everything from strategy-building to storytelling.

He began podcasting in 2018, which led to the creation of this book, and to date has produced over 600 podcast episodes within the shows, "The Daily Undoing" and "Background Noise."

David's personal life revolves around his family; wife Anne-Marie and children Eva and Gabby. When not hanging with them he can be found before dawn's early light maintaining a somewhat psychotic running regimen, or ducking out for a motorcycle ride (usually in the daylight).